Justin — Live your dreams, love your passion!.
Best.
Hunter

5-

D1109459

They embrace the new reality of customer-centric IT. From my perspective, it's all part of the big shift—the transformation of IT from an inward-looking technology function to an outward-looking business process that drives and enables real value for the modern enterprise.

CIO Focus Shifts from Creating Internal Productivity to Driving External Value

I had an excellent conversation with my friend Mike Fitz, vice president of business solutions at Sprint, about the business impact of the big shift in CIO leadership and how the changing focus of IT is helping more companies drive new revenue in competitive markets.

"The role of the CIO is evolving from an internal focus on employee productivity to an external focus on growing the business," Mike says. "It's not a total break with the past. CIOs are still interested in helping employees become more productive through better use of technology. That hasn't changed. But what has changed dramatically is that more CIOs are stepping up and using new technology to drive revenue for their companies. That's the big shift, from our perspective."

Social media, big data, cloud, and mobile have been game changers. But those newer technologies have also raised the bar, and expectations are now significantly higher than in the past. "Ten or 15 years ago, the CIO could say, 'Wow, look at how many of our employees have e-mail,' and it would have been a big deal. Today, it's not such a big deal. The modern

CIO has 'graduated' from providing technology just for the sake of improved productivity," Mike says.

I think that Mike makes an excellent point. The idea of building a business on productivity by itself has become an old-fashioned idea. That's not to say that productivity isn't important—but the modern enterprise relies on more than productivity to achieve long-term business success in competitive markets.

"That realization has created some great business opportunities for us here at Sprint," Mike says. "We offer turnkey capabilities that enable CIOs to help employees become more productive. We also offer technologies and services that help companies grow their revenue."

From my perspective, the "bifurcated" approach developed by Mike and his team represents a highly logical response to the genuine needs of modern CIOs. It clearly reflects the progression of IT leadership as it evolves from focusing purely on productivity enhancements to focusing more broadly on achieving business results that are aligned with enterprise strategy.

Mike has captured the essence of the shift in IT leadership. Today's CIO is much more than a technology person engaged in a series of either/or scenarios. The modern CIO operates in full partnership with the C-suite, and is perceived as a valuable source of expert knowledge that is applied primarily to growing the business. Productivity is still important, but generating revenue for the enterprise has become the CIO's preeminent focus.

Competitive Success Is Linked to Collaboration and Innovation

GE Global Innovation Barometer 2014, issued in mid-2014, reveals a key shift in attitude among top executives. Unlike previous surveys, the new study shows that executives seem ready to take greater risks in the race for competitive advantage. The report is definitely worth reading, and it confirms my informal observations over the past 24 months.

There's definitely a strong consensus emerging about the critical links between collaboration, innovation, and market success. The report also supports the idea of the big shift, in which companies focus the bulk of their energy and attention on creating excellent experiences for their customers, particularly in highly competitive and rapidly evolving markets.

"Executives believe that efficient and successful innovation hinges on three factors: understanding customers and anticipating market evolutions (84%); attracting and retaining the most talented and skilled employees (79%); and quickly adopting emerging technologies (67%)," the report states.[3]

The report notes that "big data has evolved from a buzzword to an important tool in the innovation process, albeit one that executives recognize poses certain difficulties.

While 70% of businesses see big data as critical to optimize business efficiency, 61% believe it will be a real challenge to implement. For those who utilize it, 69% see added value for the innovation process."[4]

Frankly, most of the CIOs and IT leaders I speak with have already invested in some form of advanced analytics that feed on big data sources. Almost everyone I meet is interested in learning more about big data and the technologies around it.

The report also touches on the potential impact of the Internet of Things (IoT), which GE often refers to as the *Industrial Internet,* or the concept that anything electronic can be connected to the Internet. Whatever you call it, the phenomenon is growing quickly and will soon become inescapable. Some experts predict that by the end of 2020, the IoT will connect 212 billion "things," ranging from diesel locomotives and jet engines to thermostats and refrigerators.

"The Industrial Internet is an emerging concept but positively received, with half agreeing that it will drive innovation success in the future. But only one in four feels prepared to use it," according to the GE report.

There are numerous opportunities here for IT leaders who are willing to seize them. Will you be ready when those opportunities arise? The key to readiness is fairly straightforward: You need to understand the relationship between collaboration, innovation, and competitive success, and then make sure you have the pieces in place to move forward with speed and confidence.

Shifting Consumer Demands Require CIOs to Adjust to the Experience Economy

Most of what I've written about the big shift in IT leadership has focused on the changing relationships between the CIO and other key executives in the enterprise.

The big shift, however, is driven by fundamental changes in the broader economy, and it's important not to lose sight of the bigger picture. From a high-level perspective, the big shift is one element in a gradual transformation of the globalized consumer economy away from products and toward experiences.

As consumers shift their attention from buying products to buying experiences, the focus of the enterprise also must shift. For the CIO, the shift from a product-based economy to an experience-based economy represents a challenge of truly epic proportions. It's no longer enough for a company to offer great products or services—now it must also offer great experiences.

Empowered consumers have higher demands. Armed with personal computers (PCs), laptops, and mobile devices, customers can reach out and touch any company at any time of night or day. That means that companies must be ready to meet the expectations of their customers on a 24/7/365 basis. In the networked consumer economy, downtime is intolerable.

The notion of zero downtime puts enormous pressure on the CIO to deliver flawless IT around the clock. Suddenly, the CIO has a much heavier burden and, truthfully, many CIOs seem unprepared.

When I entered the industry, the role of IT was primarily focused on helping the accounting department close its books and generate financial reports for the C-suite. Those days are long past, but some of us are still acting as if they might return.

Like it or not, the arrow of time only flies in one direction. We have to get ourselves accustomed to the new environment of empowered consumers and their elevated demands. The good news is that the *experience economy* actually plays to the strengths of IT, since many of the experiences that customer demand can only be delivered through advanced digital technologies.

As IT leaders, we need to do a better job of aligning ourselves with our peers in research and development, product development, manufacturing, marketing, sales, distribution, and service—those are the parts of the enterprise that really need our help and expertise.

We have a lot to offer. But we've got to step up and join the battle. The good old days are gone. We've got to offer creative and effective solutions for dealing with the realities of the present, or we'll quickly become part of the past.

Shifting Consumer Economy Raises the Bar for CIOs

The transformation of the consumer economy away from products and toward experiences isn't merely an interesting phenomenon—it will require a corresponding shift in how CIOs plan strategy and lead their organizations.

I strongly believe that shift in strategy and leadership could easily become the most profound and long-lasting transformation in the history of information technology industry.

Here's why: Delivering great products is easier than delivering great experiences. Once a product is manufactured, it's probably going to work as advertised until it breaks or wears out. When you focus on experiences, however, you need to deliver a product (whether it's made of atoms or electrons) that works and delights the consumer. Suddenly, the bar for success is much higher.

CIOs will be involved intimately in the process of helping their companies meet those new—and significantly higher—levels of consumer expectations. CIOs must be prepared to help their companies achieve those newer and higher levels, or suffer the consequences.

Until very recently, the typical buying experience began with consumers going to stores or shopping malls and physically interacting with products. For most consumers, the buying experience no longer works that way.

Today, the modern consumer experience begins on a laptop or mobile device. That means that the typical consumer begins his or her relationship with your company by interacting with IT. It is not a stretch or an exaggeration to say that IT has become the store. In fact, it's become the whole store! Consumers not only interact with products from their laptops or mobile devices, they change the colors and sizes, they "try them on," they choose the speed and method by which they are delivered, and, of course, they pay for them via credit, debit, or a variety of new payment technologies.

Two years ago, CIOs were satisfied to help their companies complete transactions online. Today, the expectations are much higher. In addition to enabling simple sales transactions, CIOs must help their companies digitize all of the steps required for a successful consumer experience. It's a long and highly fluid process that includes product design, materials sourcing, manufacturing, marketing, sales, fulfillment, and customer support.

It's a tall order, but that's the new reality of the big shift in consumerism. In the modern economy, the CIO is absolutely indispensable and critical to the success of the business. Are you ready to leap over the higher bar?

Case Closed: IT Still Matters

As most of us know, Nicholas Carr wrote an article in 2003 titled "IT Doesn't Matter," followed by a book in 2004 titled *Does IT Matter?*[5] For years, it was common for people in the IT industry to debate the accuracy of Carr's vision and to question to the relevancy of the IT function.

Thankfully, I think we can agree today that the matter is settled. IT does matter, and it matters more than ever. When Carr wrote his article and book, very few people were thinking about the long-term effects of newer technology trends such as cloud, mobile, and social. Outside of Google, almost nobody was considering the impact of big data on IT infrastructure. The term *Internet of Things* hadn't been invented, and few people believed that machine-to-machine (M2M) interactions would contribute significantly to Internet traffic.

Most important, Carr failed to anticipate the enormous impact of the consumerization of advanced technology. Nobody, including Carr, foresaw the mobile revolution. I don't think that Steve Jobs even realized how radically the iPhone would change the world. The incredibly rapid adoption of mobile devices has profoundly transformed the way we look at technology. Far from killing IT, consumerization has made IT even more central to our lives!

Does IT still matter? Yes, most definitely, and more than ever before. From my perspective, the outcome of business competition is determined to a major extent by technology, either directly or indirectly. Great CIOs leverage new technologies to create strong competitive advantages in rapidly changing global markets. They also take a proactive role in leading the transformation from internally focused IT to customer-centric, socially connected information platforms that drive revenue and generate real value for the business.

I think it's fair to say that IT is more relevant and more necessary now than it was 10 years ago. Ten years ago, IT still operated largely within the boundaries of the enterprise. Today, we all compete in markets that are driven by technology-savvy customers. Those customers expect and demand the best that technology can offer. IT isn't just one piece of a process—we're a core part of the solution! We are the strategy, and we will deliver the results the business needs.

Think about how much the world has changed since Carr wrote that article. Those of us in the IT industry are riding a truly unique wave of innovation and transformation. Let's enjoy the ride!

Notes

1. See "Moving from the Back Office to the Front Lines," CIO Insights from the Global C-Suite Study, © IBM Corporation 2013. Available at http://public.dhe.ibm.com/common/ssi/ecm/gb/en/gbe03580usen/GBE03580USEN.PDF.

2. For more information, read this short article from MIT Technology Review. Antonio Regalado, "Technology Is Wiping Out Companies Faster than Ever," MIT Technology Review (September 10, 2013), http://www.technologyreview.com/view/519226/technology-is-wiping-out-companies-faster-than-ever/.

3. Ideas Lab, GE Global Innovation Barometer 2014, © General Electric Company 2014, http://www.ideas laboratory.com/projects/innovation-barometer-2014/.

4. Ibid.

5. See Nicholas Carr, *"IT Doesn't Matter,"* Harvard Business Review (July 2003), and Does IT Matter? Information Technology and the Corrosion of Competitive Advantage (Boston: Harvard Business School Publishing, 2004).

Chapter 2

The CIO and the C-Suite

EXECUTIVE SUMMARY

For CIOs, relationships with senior executives across the enterprise, in the C-suite, and on the board of directors are essential. Great CIOs are constantly building social bridges across the enterprise and seeking opportunities to deepen trust with members of the corporate leadership team.

My friend Bruce Leidal is the chief information officer (CIO) at Carestream Health, Inc., a worldwide provider of dental and medical imaging systems and IT solutions; X-ray imaging systems for nondestructive testing; and advanced materials for the precision films and electronics markets.

Bruce leads Carestream Health's global information technology (IT) organization. Like many CIOs, his primary mission includes building a more efficient and effective IT organization, streamlining processes, reducing costs, and, ultimately, providing information that enables Carestream Health to optimize its business while continually improving its customers' experience.

From my perspective, Bruce is a role model for modern CIOs who successfully blend technical expertise with truly excellent corporate executive leadership skills. Bruce's ability to serve as both a technology leader and a corporate leader is exemplary.

I asked Bruce recently about the importance of building trust and establishing great working relationships across the C-suite. Specifically, I asked him about gathering input from the C-suite on a regular basis. His reply was incredibly useful, and I want to share it with you.

"I've established a group inside of IT that we call the relationship managers," says Bruce. "It's basically a sensing organization, and its job is figuring out two fundamental items: (1) What is the business trying to do strategy-wise, and how can IT to help the business achieve those strategies? (2) What are the pain points, and what can we do from an IT standpoint to help alleviate that pain? Those two factors drive our view of what IT can accomplish on behalf of our business going forward."

Input from the enterprise architecture team is also included to make sure that the most appropriate technology is deployed and the IT vision remains firmly aligned with the needs of the business.

I love how Bruce describes the relationship managers as a "sensing team," because it shows that he understands the critical importance of staying connected and aligned with the business. In my experience, the best leaders are always searching for signals, and always looking for new ways to deliver value to the enterprise.

I am especially impressed with Bruce's commitment to the "sensing" process. It's not just a one-time event—it's an ongoing practice.

"I sit down every quarter with the relationship manager who is responsible for a business area and one of my executive leadership team peers. We talk about how we're doing around service levels, how we're doing around projects. We have a strategic planning horizon—a roadmap of over three years. We talk about how that's progressing and what remains to be done. We also review satisfaction with IT. All of those components help us stay aligned and relevant to the business," says Bruce.

Clearly, Bruce has developed a practical and repeatable process for staying aligned with the business and with the C-suite. It's a winning formula and a great example of leadership excellence.

Speaking the Language of Business Is Essential for Exceptional CIOs and IT Leaders

It is critically important for CIOs to speak the language of the board and the language of the CEO when presenting to the upper echelons of the enterprise. But only a handful of CIOs seem truly comfortable speaking the "language" of top management.

I recently asked my friend Vic Bhagat to tell me how CIOs can improve their abilities to communicate effectively with senior management and boards of directors. A 30-year industry veteran, Vic is executive vice president of Enterprise Business Solutions and the CIO at EMC Corporation. With revenues of $23.2 billion in 2013 and more than 62,000 employees worldwide, EMC is a global leader in enabling businesses and service providers to transform their operations and deliver IT as a service.

His advice for CIOs is absolutely spot-on and incredibly valuable. "You have to talk in business terms: How are we going to help accelerate growth? What's the target for market share? How can IT add value by delivering analytics that drive growth? Those are questions you've got to ask," says Vic.

Earlier in his career, Vic served as CIO for multiple GE organizations, including GE Aviation Services, GE Global Growth and Operations, CNBC, GE Corporate, and GE India and Southeast Asia. In addition to driving GE's IT strategies, Vic managed large, global shared service applications; built a technology center focused on high-end technology and digital solutions; and fueled GE's global innovation by opening numerous centers of excellence focused on big data, digital analytics, and digital strategies.

It's fair to say that Vic's experience at GE, and later at Accenture, honed his business skills to an unparalleled level. When he talks about "speaking the language of business," he really means business!

"Whether you're talking to someone from sales, marketing, finance, or product development, you have to speak their language and understand their processes to drive cycle time reduction," says Vic. "If it's sales, you're talking about reducing the cycle time between a customer's inquiry and placing an order. If it's the finance team, you're talking about reducing the cycle time from when a customer places an order and the company actually collects the cash. Your dialogue has to change, depending on the audience. You cannot be talking about IT. Today, the business expects your technology to work. So you've got to talk about delivering business results."

Vic's insight is remarkably clear and exceptionally relevant. As IT professionals, it's natural that we find the technology fascinating. But as senior corporate executives, we need to demonstrate that we understand the needs and goals of the business. Speaking the language of business is a huge step in the right direction.

Leverage the Power of Great Habits to Drive Relationships across the C-Suite

Successful CIOs create and sustain great working relationships across the C-suite. They turn relationship-building into a habit, and they recognize opportunities for deepening the bonds that are essential for success at the executive level of the enterprise.

One of my friends is the CIO of a very large and well-known tech company. He makes it a habit to take his boss to lunch on a regular basis. He makes sure the lunch is relaxed and informal. He picks restaurants that feature the kind of food the boss likes. My friend avoids asking for favors or making requests during the lunch. That way, the boss won't be looking for a reason to skip the next lunch!

Another of my friends is the CIO of a privately held company operating in a tightly regulated industry. Although he reports directly to the CEO, the executive board is very active in the company's decision-making processes. My friend makes it a habit to meet regularly with the board. He also meets regularly with the board's audit committee, which plays a key role in monitoring compliance. He makes sure that his reports and presentation are written in the language used by the board members. He demonstrates clearly that he understands their goals and objectives.

Working directly with the board and its committees has become a habit for my friend. As a result of the relationships he has developed, he is rarely surprised or blindsided by decisions from the C-suite. He can react more swiftly and more effectively when the C-suite needs something done in a hurry. That makes him an irreplaceable asset to the enterprise.

Both friends have developed great habits that support and drive their success as executives at major companies. The more time that I spend in this field, the more I appreciate the value of developing good habits. Most of you have read *The 7 Habits of Highly Effective People* by Stephen R. Covey. I also want to recommend another book, *The Power of Habit: Why We Do What We Do in Life and Business*, by Charles Duhigg.[1]

Duhigg became interested in the power of habit when he was a reporter in Iraq. He writes about how the US military was able to stop a series of deadly riots in a small city's main plaza by simply changing one aspect of the city's culture. Here's the story: An Army major noticed that many of the rioters were eating food provided by vendors in the plaza.

Eating food in the plaza during a riot had become part of their habit. The major asked the city's mayor to prohibit vendors from selling food in the plaza. As soon as the food vendors disappeared, the rioters stopped coming to the plaza.

I love that story because it shows so clearly that we can leverage the power of habits to change the world around us. One observant officer figured out how to stop the riots, without firing a shot.

If you look around your organization, I'm sure that you can identify habits that will help you drive your agenda and achieve your objectives as an executive. You can also identify habits that are holding you back or making it harder for your team to reach its goals.

Maintain Relevancy and Set the Agenda

I recently had an incredibly valuable conversation with Tim McCabe, former senior vice president and CIO at Delphi Automotive, a leading global supplier of technologies for the automotive and commercial vehicle markets. Headquartered in Gillingham, England, Delphi operates major technical centers, manufacturing sites, and customer support services in 32 countries, with regional headquarters in Luxembourg, Brazil, China, and the United States.

During our conversation, Tim shared his insight and experience around a key challenge facing almost every modern CIO: developing great working relationships with the top executives who manage the firm and with the boards that provide guidance and advice.

As I've written before, it's absolutely essential for the CIO to build deep and trusting relationships across the C-suite and in the boardroom. Tim delineated four major reasons for taking the time and making the effort required to build high-quality relationships at the highest levels of the firm:

1. Maintaining the relevancy of IT

2. Assuring that IT sets the IT agenda

3. Maintaining organizational and positional authority necessary for executing enterprise-wide transformation

4. Knowing where you stand with the firm's topmost leaders and influencers

"If you're too far removed from top management, things can get lost in translation and you might not get the message they're trying to deliver," says Tim. "So first and foremost, you've got to assure what you're doing is relevant and aligns with the CEO's vision."

Setting the agenda is also critical. "When something is communicated by someone else on your behalf, the context can be lost," Tim explains. "The best way to own the IT agenda is by taking it directly to the CEO and the board."

Working directly with top executives offers the opportunity to build deeper bonds of trust and heighten their confidence in your abilities. That trust and confidence "will come in handy when you are executing on a major transformation that might be unpopular with some people," says Tim.

In addition to providing direct exposure to strategy at the highest levels, interacting with senior management and board members will raise your visibility within the organization. "You have to cross that Rubicon at some point in your career, and it's always better to know where you stand with the executive leadership," he says.

Working with a board of directors can be especially useful, since most directors are current or former CEOs, and they are accustomed to working with CIOs. "They tend to have a broad set of experiences and they've seen a variety of IT projects, both good and bad. They can be great sources of information and advice," says Tim.

Tim's advice is exceptionally valuable for all IT leaders at every level of the organization. Great leaders are constantly learning, and one of the best ways to learn is by interacting with seasoned executives and directors.

Team Leaders Are Not Lone Heroes

The lone hero galloping to the rescue is a common image in movies. In real life, however, great team leaders are more valuable than dashing lone heroes. In real life—and especially in a large enterprise—team leaders are the people who help the organization move forward through collaboration and cooperation. Lone heroes, on the other hand, tend to generate resentment and disunity. As a result, their quests often end in failure.

In today's modern enterprise, CIOs need to focus on being great team leaders. Patrick Steele, the former executive vice president and CIO at Delta Dental of California, reminded me of that simple but important truth in a recent conversation.

"You need the ability to network across the C-suite. You need to get the business leaders involved so they feel a sense of ownership. You have to move within the framework of the organization. If you ride in like a superstar cowboy, you might not get invited to sit around the campfire," says Patrick.

I really like how Patrick frames his primary responsibilities in terms of leadership, and not technical expertise. "You need to figure out ways to inspire trust and encourage involvement. If you try to do it all by yourself, you'll inspire resentment, especially if you're a newcomer. That's human nature. You have to accept it and learn to work within the realities of the business," says Patrick.

At the same time, if you're hired to be an agent of change, you can't sit back and let the status quo remain unchallenged. "You should be an aggressive catalyst for change," says Patrick. "And make sure the business has skin in the game so they have a reason to help you."

You also have to deliver results, of course. But that's a given. Most important, you need to think and act like a leader. I love how Patrick describes his role as an "aggressive catalyst." I think those words capture the idea perfectly. A catalyst allows other elements to mix and to react, forming a new compound. That's exactly what a great CIO does.

Leaders Need "Triple Package" of Critical Traits

I read an excellent op-ed column in the *New York Times* about the drivers of success.[2] The column described how different cultures prepare their children for success, but it just as easily could have been written about IT leaders in the modern enterprise.

The authors observe that "strikingly successful groups in America today share three traits that, together, propel success. The first is a superiority complex—a deep-seated belief in their exceptionality. The second appears to be the opposite—insecurity, a feeling that you or what you've done is not good enough. The third is impulse control."

The authors refer to the three traits as the *triple package*, and it strikes me as a highly accurate description of the "soft skills" required for successful executive leadership in today's hyper-competitive business environments. Let's unpack the concept and see how it applies to IT leaders.

First, great IT leaders are confident and secure. They believe deeply and sincerely in their abilities to analyze difficult problems and devise elegant solutions, quickly and effectively.

Second, they tend to be strivers—the best IT leaders I know are people who are always looking for ways to do their job better. They are never quite satisfied; they always want to take the game to the next level.

Third, they are patient. They don't rush into something just because everyone else thinks it's cool. They resist grasping for the next "shiny object" that comes into view. They are calm, cool, and disciplined. Sometimes their scientific approach to solving problems irritates their colleagues, but it's a critical factor in their success. They don't run off half-cocked; they wait and make sure they've considered all the angles before investing the company's money in a new technology.

Sometimes their patience and discipline are mistaken for timidity and arrogance. But the truth is that great IT leaders see themselves as trusted stewards of the company's valuable resources. They avoid making mistakes because they know the risks and the downsides. They aren't fearful; they are careful.

Great IT leaders are exceptional people. They have strength, courage, and patience. They succeed because they combine a variety of key personality traits—the "soft skills" we often talk about when we describe visionary executives.

I'm proud to work with such talented people. It's an honor and a privilege. Together, we are shaping the future of IT and empowering a new era of economic growth.

In Changing Times, Innovative Leadership Is a Critical Asset

Global business news networks recently carried two interesting stories, both supremely relevant to senior IT leaders and executives. One story was about the infamous 2013 security breach at Target. Apparently, the company's $1.6 million anti-hacker solution actually detected the breach and sent alerts to its security teams. But for a variety of reasons, according to *Bloomberg Businessweek*,[3] management did not react immediately to the alerts. In the words of a commentator, "It's like your smoke detector goes off and you respond by taking out the battery."

The security technology that Target installed worked fine, but the people and processes, it seems, weren't up to the task. There's been some speculation that people had become so accustomed to false alarms sent by previous generations of security systems that when a real alarm was sent by a more effective system, the significance of the alarm was downplayed.

There's a clear message here for all of us in IT leadership. It's not enough to purchase and install the latest and greatest technology. You also need to develop the people and processes necessary for making certain the technology delivers on your expectations.

In the past, buying and installing new enterprise systems took years. It wasn't uncommon for an enterprise resource planning (ERP) project to last longer than the tenure of the CIO who got it started. When something went wrong, a new CIO was hired to fix it.

Today, new systems can be rolled out in months or weeks. The same CIO who launched the project is expected to finish it, and that means taking responsibility for making sure that it works as advertised. The quality of your new technology alone isn't enough to guarantee success—you also need the people and processes to keep it running.

The second story that caught my attention was this: Google's revenue from desktop search dropped at the same time that its revenue from mobile search is climbing. People have been talking about the shift in ad spend from desktop computers to mobile devices, but it was fascinating to see the numbers. Rolfe Winkler's post in the *Wall Street Journal* showed that the shift from desktop to mobile is accelerating, and that will have a huge impact on IT everywhere.[4]

Are you ready for the day when everything is mobile? Are you optimizing your apps for mobile? Is your mobile app development ecosystem up and running? The days of desktop dominance are waning fast. Your customers—both internal and external—will expect the same level of oper-ability and user-friendliness from your mobile apps as they expect from your desktop apps. Are you prepared to deliver the user experiences they demand?

These are genuinely exciting times for IT leaders every-where. If there's a takeaway from the headlines, it's that great technology can only take you so far. You also need the people and processes in place to make it all work. Truly excellent IT leaders understand the critical importance of holistic strategies that leverage the full potential of human capital and new technology. Innovative leadership will almost always trump great technology, even in our current era of rapid change and global transformation.

Are You Proactive or Reactive?

My friend David Wright is the chief strategy officer at ServiceNow, the enterprise IT cloud company. Before joining ServiceNow, he served as vice president of technical services at VMware. His experience and insight give him a firm grasp of the challenges and opportunities presented by the evolution of IT into a trusted service provider for the enterprise.

We spoke recently about the opportunities for CIOs to reposition the traditional IT department as a nimble service organization. Often, the ability to make the transition depends on the CIO.

"I find there are two distinct types of CIOs: the reactive CIO and the proactive CIO," says Dave. "The reactive CIO is told, 'we need this piece of software to perform this function in our business, and you guys need to support it.' The proactive CIO is someone who develops business relationships across the C-suite and the board."

Historically, CIOs were only brought into board meetings when something went badly wrong. That's no longer the case today, says Dave. "Proactive CIOs participate in board meetings because they are perceived as being essential to the business. They've made the leap from being order-takers to being partners. They're closer and more aligned with the business than their predecessors."

From my perspective, this makes perfect sense. The closer IT gets to the business, the more indispensable it becomes. Ideally, IT and the business should be inseparable. "When IT is the business, then anything that happens in IT has a direct impact on the business," says Dave. When IT is absolutely integral to the business, the CIO becomes an essential player on the executive team.

"Top executives don't buy technology because it's cool or trendy," says Dave. "They buy technology because it fundamentally improves their business."

One way for CIOs to move closer to the business is by supporting and enabling an enterprise service platform. For example, IT can provide an enterprise-wide portal that would allow employees to access services (such as legal, travel, and HR) directly from their laptops or mobile devices. IT already has the experience and capabilities required to develop and maintain an enterprise-wide service system, so why not just do it?

"IT already has the best-practices and the framework for providing an enterprise service platform," says Dave. "IT can also take a leadership role in developing an enterprise-wide catalog of services. That's something that most departments wouldn't naturally do, but it's natural for IT."

The immediate benefit of such a system would be a reduction in e-mail traffic. But the real economic value of an enterprise service platform is that it allows the enterprise to measure precisely when, where and how services are consumed. Results can be displayed on a dashboard; services can be monitored for usage, effectiveness, and quality. Most important, services can be optimized and improved.

"It actually ends up making everyone's life easier," says Dave. "For the most part, you can use existing IT systems to get the job done. From the IT perspective, you're taking complex processes and simplifying them for the business, without adding overhead or buying lots of new technology. Proactive CIOs see that as a win-win scenario, on many levels."

I genuinely appreciate how Dave envisions the role of the proactive CIO in the modern enterprise, and I'm glad he took the time to share his thoughts about the value of creating enterprise-wide service platforms.

Leaders Build Trust, across the C-Suite and within

The speed of change continues accelerating at an astonishing tempo. Clinging to the past is not a viable strategy. As a sailor, I learned that it makes no sense to fight the wind. When you're sailing, you gauge the wind and put it to work for you.

Successful CIOs understand that IT must become more nimble, more flexible, and more agile. In today's connected economy, speed is everything. Speed is expected. It's become an essential and irreplaceable component of customer service. It's a foundational part of operational excellence. Without speed, the company cannot remain competitive.

Speed, flexibility, and agility also require higher levels of trust and deeper partnerships with peers across the C-suite. Learning to move rapidly is only part of the story—we also need to learn how to move together smoothly, in perfect synchronization and harmony.

Building trusted relationships across the C-suite has become an absolutely critical part of the CIO's role. Building a great leadership team within IT is equally important. You need a deep bench of talented players to keep a winning streak going!

Preparing for the Future of IT Includes Waging the War for Talent

As I wrote earlier, IT matters more than ever to the overall health of the modern enterprise. Technology drives economic growth and development, and IT is still the place where technology and business come together.

That said, the extreme pace of technological change has caught many organizations off guard. Everyone is talking about cloud, mobile, social, big data and the Internet of Things, but relatively few IT leaders have taken the steps necessary to prepare their IT teams for tomorrow's challenges.

From my perspective, the first step is always creating a vision for the future. The next step is developing a strategy for bringing that vision into reality. The third—and absolutely critical—step is assembling the people, process, and technology that will enable the strategy and drive it forward.

When you look at that trio—people, process, and technology—the easiest part is the technology. Most of the technology needed to support truly data-intensive business strategies already exists. The process piece is also well understood and generally accepted. The piece of the strategic puzzle that's missing is people. That's why so many executives I know are talking earnestly and intensely about the looming war for talent.

People with the skills, abilities, experience, and character to get the job done are in short supply. Large companies compete fiercely for top talent, making it even harder for smaller firms to find and hire the best people.

The war for talent raises many complicated questions. Where should we look for talent? Can we "grow our own" talent with the right training programs? What is the right mix of insourcing and outsourcing?

One pressing issue is developing the basic skills and capabilities required for moving ahead with big data initiatives.

Some people say that it's relatively easy for experienced database administrators (DBAs) to acquire the technical skills necessary for managing big data systems.

Others say that handling big data requires special training and new styles of leadership. Some believe those skills and abilities can be taught in-house, while others aren't so sure. Some people say that universities are the best places to look for data scientists, while others say that genuine business experience will always trump great technical skills.

It's hard to predict the future, but that doesn't relieve us from our responsibilities for envisioning that path forward and taking the steps needed to prepare the enterprise for a world in which IT will matter more than ever before.

Find the Best People—You'll Need Them as IT Expands Its Role

I have extensively written about the "war for talent" and the critical importance of focusing resources on finding the best people for IT.

It's no secret that large companies have the resources to find and acquire top talent. Based on simple math, you would think the best people work at the largest companies. But in IT, you often find the best and the brightest at smaller firms. Why is that?

Part of the answer is that money isn't everything. The younger generation looks for a collaborative work environment that offers a sense of purpose, a spirit of community, and a fulfilling career.

As an IT leader, you have to ask yourself if you've created a work environment that not only attracts top talent but also retains top talent. Moreover, you need to be honest with yourself about the quality of your mid-level managers. Are they encouraging and nurturing new hires, or are they undermining them?

Anyone who has played a competitive team sport knows the nervous feeling of watching a new crop of players arrive. Rightly or wrongly, you feel certain that one of them will replace you, and you'll wind up sitting on the bench. That kind of anxiety is common. Great coaches understand it, and they provide moral support for their veteran players. That doesn't mean that great coaches never replace veteran players—it means that great coaches focus on the whole team, not just the rookies or the veterans.

The best CIOs make sure their deputies and managers understand that IT is a genuine team effort, and that every individual on the team can make an impact. Older and more seasoned members of the team have different needs than younger and less experienced members of the team. Someone who graduated from college in 1993 relates to technology differently than someone who graduated from college in 2013. Managers and directors must take those differences into account or risk alienating entire groups of workers.

IT resources are limited, and salaries account for a large portion of every IT budget. Successful IT leaders invest the time and energy necessary to figure out what motivates their employees—and they do everything they can to retain the top talent they acquire. It takes a couple of years for new hires to hit their stride, so it makes good business sense to keep them engaged and motivated, especially when they're new on the job.

Achieving the Right Mix of Talent and Technical Abilities

As the CIO evolves from a service provider to a value creator, the mix of human capital in the IT organization is also changing. While the need for technical expertise is still important, there is an increasing need for new hires with a blend of technical ability, business acumen, and interpersonal skills.

There's also a push for creating work environments that reflect the needs and expectations of younger workers and digital natives who grew up with smartphones and social media. Higher levels of transparency and openness are becoming the norm across virtually all sectors of the economy.

Ten years ago, the best CIOs focused on transforming the state of enterprise IT. Now they are focused on transforming the IT organization itself. In many respects, the challenges of yesterday and today are similar. The great CIOs understand that transformation depends on changing people, processes, and technology. All three must be addressed to achieve change that is truly transformational.

I spoke recently to Rich Adduci, senior vice president and CIO at Boston Scientific Corporation. Rich is a great guy and a brilliant IT leader. He sees the war for talent as a major focus of the modern CIO, and he articulates the challenge clearly. "We have to develop the next generation of leaders," says Rich. "We need people who fundamentally think differently about IT and its role in the enterprise."

From Rich's perspective, talent is the new frontier. "That's where my executive team will be spending a lot of its energy," says Rich. "For some, this is going to be a break from the past. We're shifting the primary focus of IT from developing technology to developing competitive advantages for the company. It's going to require a different set of skills and capabilities. We're trying to develop those skills in-house, and we're also looking outside the organization. We're building a pipeline so we can tap into the skills we need as an organization."

I am genuinely impressed by Rich's vision. In addition to his passion and enthusiasm, he brings deep knowledge and experience to the table. He's not just talking; he's designing and implementing the future state of the IT organization.

"It's not an either/or situation. IT organizations need people who combine superior technology skills with great business leadership skills," says Rich. "There's been a tendency to assume that all the technology has been commoditized. But that's simply not true. We still need great technology people, and we also need people who understand how businesses compete in the modern world. It's an added dimension, and it's essential.

I agree with Rich. Today's successful CIOs work closely with their executive teams to make certain that their IT organizations have the right mix of talent and capabilities. As Rich says, it's not a case of either/or. Top-tier IT teams hire and retain top performers who understand the fundamentals of technology and the essence of business competition.

Why I'm Genuinely Optimistic about the Future of IT

The tech economy is already huge and still growing. Technology spending is up almost everywhere. There are lots of good reasons for the continued upsurge in tech spending, but the primary driver is return on investment (ROI). Technology is a great investment, even in a turbulent and unpredictable economy.

For CIOs and IT leaders, the good news is that virtually all of that new technology is connected to the IT grid. Even if the new technology your company buys isn't technically IT, all new technology will need to interface at some point with your IT infrastructure. From that moment on, it becomes another node in the greater IT universe, and that makes it another item in the CIO's expanding portfolio of responsibilities.

So whether you call it tech or you call it IT, it will become part of the CIO's domain, probably sooner than later. From my perspective, that's not just good news—it's great news! The notion that IT is going away or becoming irrelevant is simply false. To the contrary, IT is becoming more important and more indispensable than ever before.

Recently *Computerworld* ran an article with the headline, "Tech Hiring Accounts for 10% of U.S. Employment Gains."[5] That headline should not surprise anyone in our industry. What did surprise me, however, was a quote in the article from a labor analyst saying that CIOs don't plan to hire new staff.

The CIOs I speak with are generally very positive about the tech economy and see a bright future in their expanding roles as full-fledged executive leaders. They are also aware that newer technologies such as cloud, social, mobile, and big data analytics require hiring new people with different skills. To me, that suggests that IT is poised for a hiring surge to meet what will certainly be strong demand for new capabilities based on the new technologies.

Instead of making IT irrelevant, the consumerization of advanced technology has made IT even more critical and definitely elevated the role of the CIO as a key executive in the enterprise. When viewed in the aggregate, all of this points to the beginning of another great period for IT development and leadership.

Notes

1. See Stephen Covey, *The 7 Habits of Highly Effective People* (New York: Simon & Schuster, 2004); and Charles Duhigg, *The Power of Habit: Why We Do What We Do in Life and Business* (New York: Random House, 2014).

2. Amy Chua and Jed Rubenfeldjan, "What Drives Success?" *The New York Times* (January 25, 2014), http://www.nytimes.com/2014/01/26/opinion/sunday/what-drives-success.html?action=click&module=Search&region=searchResults%230&version=&url=http%3A%2F%2Fquery.nytimes.com%2Fsearch%2Fsitesearch%2F%3Faction%3Dclick%26region%3DMasthead%26pgtype%3DHomepage%26mo&_r=0.

3. Michael Riley, Ben Elgin, Dune Lawrence, and Carol Matlack, "Missed Alarms and 40 Million Stolen Credit Card Numbers: How Target Blew It," *BloombergBusinessweek* (March 13, 2014), http://www.businessweek.com/articles/2014-03-13/target-missed-alarms-in-epic-hack-of-credit-card-data#r=hp-sf.

4. Rolfe Winkler, "As Desktop Declines, Mobile Search Boosts Google Revenue," *WSJ.D*, (March 13, 2014), http://blogs.wsj.com/digits/2014/03/13/as-desktop-declines-mobile-search-boosts-google-revenue/?mod=ST1.

5. Patrick Thiodeau, "Tech Hiring Accounts for 10% of U.S. Employment Gains," *Computerworld* (July 8, 2013), http://www.computerworld.com/article/2483611/it-careers/tech-hiring-accounts-for-10--of-u-s--employment-gains.html.

Chapter 3

Innovation

EXECUTIVE SUMMARY

Innovation is required to create and maintain competitive advantages in swiftly changing markets. But innovation is difficult to manage; establishing a culture of innovation requires true leadership skills and a talent for picking winners from a crowded field. Great CIOs achieve a balance between continuous innovation and operational excellence, which are both required for steady business growth.

As I was interviewing about a dozen chief information officers (CIOs) for this book project, I began noticing a pattern in the ways that CIOs define innovation.

Successful CIOs make sure that their definitions of innovation correspond closely to the definitions used by the company's senior business leaders. The best CIOs listen carefully to how the business units define innovation, and then align information technology (IT) to strategy to match those definitions.

Aligning the IT perspective on innovation with the business perspective on innovation eliminates many of the hurdles that make it difficult for CIOs to deliver business-critical IT projects on budget and on time.

Achieving that kind of alignment can be challenging, however. Some CIOs find it difficult to surrender control of IT projects, and many CIOs resist efforts to define innovation in nontechnical terms.

My experience has taught me that CIOs who insist on calling all of the shots, all of the time, are usually less successful than CIOs who make consistent efforts to communicate with their executive peers and really try to understand the needs of the company's business units.

The truth is that the definition of innovation isn't set in stone. How you define innovation depends on where you're standing—if you're on the front lines of the business, innovation is going to look a lot different than it does to someone in the back office.

The key lesson here is that it's incredibly important for CIOs to understand how the business defines innovation, and to accept the fact that the business's definition will not match perfectly with an idealized or "perfect-world" version of innovation.

Since the business is usually responsible for driving revenue, successful CIOs listen carefully and adjust their definition of innovation to match the business's definition. In the modern enterprise, executive leaders must be on the same page. Since innovation is fundamentally critical to success in competitive markets, it's imperative for the enterprise to settle on a shared definition of innovation that works for the business and for IT.

To me, it seems logical for the CIO to take a leadership role in developing a common, practical definition of innovation. Based on the experiences of the successful CIOs that I've interviewed, the best way to get started is by opening honest dialogues between IT and the business units. Find out how different parts of the enterprise define innovation, and don't assume that everyone defines innovation the same way as the IT team.

Great CIOs take the time to find out how the business defines innovation, and then take the right steps to make certain that IT delivers on the business's expectations.

Great CIOs Leverage Innovation to Create New Products and Drive Real Growth for the Business

Everyone talks about innovation, but it's hard for most companies to articulate precisely what innovation means. That can lead to problems down the road, because what seems like innovation to one person can seem counterproductive or wasteful to someone else.

I recently spoke about innovation with my friend Dr. Ashwin Ballal. Ashwin is vice president and CIO at KLA-Tencor, a global leader in the manufacture of process control and yield management products for the semiconductor industry. The company also supplies essential software and products for the data storage, LED, and nanoelectronics industries.

"The word 'innovation' tends to be used very loosely," says Ash. "We prefer to talk about 'ideas-to-cash,' which describes ideas that can be turned into marketable products or services."

From his perspective, IT is uniquely positioned to offer key guidance and support for innovation designed to grow the business and generate revenue. "We have the broadest view of the enterprise. We see what's happening in the different lines of business and we understand how they operate," says Ash. "From our vantage point, we can see the possibilities for new business products and services."

Ash says that his experience as an executive with broad business and technology background makes him comfortable with the idea that "everyone in the company is responsible for helping the company grow. At some level, we're all part of sales and marketing."

All CIOs—no matter what company they work for—need to embrace the idea that they play an essential role in the company's success. "Today, every business is an IT business. The new realities of modern business have profound implications for every CIO," he says.

I totally agree. The great CIOs of today combine technology expertise with business knowledge to drive real value for the business. They use their unique vantage point to create new streams of revenue by "stitching together" the disparate silos and functions of the enterprise. They often see opportunities that cannot be easily seen by executives and leaders working within the lines of business.

At KLA-Tencor, for example, the IT team analyzes raw log data to identify possibilities for new products and services. "We've set up our own data science lab and we look for correlations in the data that yield useful insights we can pass along to the business," says Ash. "We are now engaging directly with customers, helping them optimize performance and create competitive advantages for their businesses."

IT is perfectly suited to provide the kind of practical innovation that modern companies need. The ideas-to-cash model described by Ash is the right path for every company that aspires to create and support a culture of continuous innovation and steady business growth.

CIOs Are Essential for Enabling Innovation

I recently had another great conversation with Thaddeus Arroyo, CEO of AT&T Mexico, LLC., and former chief information officer at AT&T. From my perspective, Thaddeus is a genuine IT thought leader and a true believer in the essential role of the modern CIO as focal point for converging technologies in an increasingly interconnected world.

"The evolution and convergence of multiple technologies—driven by powerful mobile computing connected to fast and ever present networks accessing services in the cloud—are accelerating innovation and productivity across many dimensions of the modern economy. The CIO is a critical player in this transformation," says Thaddeus. "Operating with tremendous visibility into every line of business and every operating unit, CIO's are positioned to be leaders in recognizing cross-organization capabilities as well as information integration opportunities that can improve the customer experience and enhance or disrupt market offerings. CIOs must not just be integrators or enablers; we must become transformation leaders."

Ultimately, says Thaddeus, the goal is maximizing the capacity of the IT organization to innovate on a continuous basis. Continuous innovation requires a functional neural system for passing information and transferring knowledge seamlessly across the enterprise. That's why IT remains absolutely essential—because IT has the experience and skills necessary to keep the neural system up and running.

"New technologies have rapidly accelerated the pace of innovation," says Thaddeus. "But to drive innovation at scale, you need to nurture a culture of innovation that supports employees in exploring and developing their ideas. At AT&T, this includes a crowd-sourced innovation engine that allows employees to vote up the best ideas for funding. Additionally, we utilize experiential-based methodologies that analyze key interactions between users, systems, and the environment, leading to proofs-of-concept that allow employees to try, fail, and improve. We strive to build these practices of innovation within the AT&T IT organization in order to make innovation part of our DNA. The result is an IT organization that aspires to serve as a progressive innovator, transforming business processes and market offerings in ways that create value and have positive impact for AT&T's business, customers, and collaborators while materially contributing to AT&T's intellectual capital growth and total patent portfolio."

In the technology-enabled landscape, information will be collected, stored, analyzed, and consumed in various ways, creating many new and exciting opportunities for improving and expanding the customer experience. "It doesn't matter what industry you're in, or whether you're a B2B or a B2C company," says Thaddeus. "The modern CIO will help the company drive innovation, create valuable new services, and drive business growth."

Thaddeus says that he sees CIOs "pivoting up" to become strategic players at the C-level. "Companies are now demanding more from their CIOs," he says. "They expect us to deliver innovation and transformation that lead to real growth and value. The upshot is that there is a tremendous opportunity for CIOs to help their business partners realize unprecedented returns on their technology investment, deliver shorter innovation cycles, and deepen their end-customer relationships."

I love the passion and enthusiasm of his message. Thaddeus talks the talk and walks the walk, having served as a great role model for IT leaders and technology executives. We've earned our seat at the table, and now it's time to deliver. I am totally confident that we will succeed!

CIOs Are Evolving from Tactical Support to Strategic Leadership

My friend Ralph Loura recently joined Hewlett-Packard as CIO for Enterprise Group and Global Sales Operations. Not long ago, I asked him to trace the evolution of the IT function from its early days as a tactical support group to its current role as a genuine leader of enterprise strategy.

"In the past, we left strategy to the business. IT was about execution, not strategy," says Ralph. "Today, IT is more involved in strategy development. We're taking more of a leadership role. In the past, relatively few CIOs were considered strategic leaders. Now it is more common for CIOs to play key roles in developing corporate strategy."

As the role of CIO evolves and broadens, new executive skills are required. "You need the ability to inspire people. It's less about management and more about leadership," says Ralph. "Good leaders know how to align teams and people, and how to rally them behind a cause. You need to get people engaged and really excited about their jobs."

The ability to look at technology from a user's perspective also helps, Ralph says. "You have to understand what people are trying to do and then try to make it easier for them. If you focus on the user-centric perspective, you're more likely to find a way to unlock more productivity from people. What you discover might not always be something that everyone else is already doing."

I think that Ralph really hits an important note here. Sometimes the most valuable innovations arise from watching how people use technology, and then really trying to understand how you can make their lives easier. I also like the way that Ralph focuses on the idea of leveraging technology innovation to unlock productivity across the enterprise. That's an area where IT can provide invaluable guidance and unparalleled leadership.

There's no question in my mind that the CIO's role is evolving toward greater strategic leadership. Ralph is the kind of CIO who has more than just a seat the table—his executive network extends across the enterprise, and he's totally aligned with the company's strategic objectives.

Leaders Create Tangible Value for the Modern Enterprise

Here's a great story that offers a great example of how innovative IT leadership generates real value. Jay Ferro is the CIO of the American Cancer Society (ACS), an organization that has worked relentlessly for more than 100 years to save lives and create a world with less cancer. With millions of supporter worldwide, the ACS helps people stay well and get well, finds cures, and battles valiantly against cancer.

When Jay joined the ACS, it was a decentralized organization with more than a dozen independent divisions. Jay was tasked with creating a unified IT function across the ACS. In many ways, his efforts would blaze a trail for the rest of the organization.

"IT was the canary in the coal mine," Jay recalls. "Our CEO's mandate was to create a unified ACS. It was a once-in-a-generation project and IT would be the first part of the larger transformation."

For the ACS, the ultimate goal is saving more lives. To achieve that goal, the organization had to become more effective and more agile. "Because we're a donor-driven organization, we need to operate as efficiently and as effectively as possible," says Jay. "We have volunteers and employees in several hundred locations around the world. They needed an IT organization with streamlined systems delivering world-class service. And of course, when you have more than 70 million donors giving their hard-earned money to move the needle in the battle against cancer, we take that very seriously."

Unifying IT wasn't easy. It required new and higher levels of standardization, simplification, efficiency, and security. "We were suboptimal in many ways. We had far too systems that were redundant and outdated. We had a lot of unmined, untapped data, sitting in disparate databases. Because of that, we were unable to derive insights about our donor base," recalls Jay.

"We did some very aggressive application infrastructure rationalizations. Today, we have one set of core processes. We have one system to match every major process. We have an enterprise data warehousing capability that we've never had before. We have near real-time access to key performance metrics. We've laid the foundation for applying advanced analytics to our data. It's been a game changer for us," says Jay.

The IT team also made strides in the adoption of mobile solutions to improve communications with volunteers in the field and to make it easier for people to donate contributions from remote locations.

"Historically, we had unintentionally created roadblocks that made it harder for people to give. For example, for a long time we didn't accept PayPal and certain types of credit cards. We didn't provide mobile solutions for managing our fundraising teams. We didn't have mobile access for reporting and account management," Jay explains. "But we have all of that now. We've made tremendous strides. For instance, we moved 11,000 accounts from Lotus Notes to Office 365. It sounds like nuts-and-bolts stuff, but it's a microcosm of our transformation. We've eliminated 50 percent of our legacy applications."

Having a simplified IT environment makes it easier for the IT team to roll out new technologies when they are needed—and helps everyone keep the momentum flowing toward a positive outcome.

Honestly, I love those kinds of success stories. Jay's achievements at ACS make me proud of our industry. Innovative IT leadership creates tangible value, and Jay's story is solid evidence that we're moving in the right direction.

Bringing the Consumer Service Experience into the Modern Global Enterprise

We've all heard the phrase *consumerization of IT* so often that it's almost become a cliché. But even though the phrase has become a cliché, the trend itself is still important and relevant to CIOs.

People are people first, and they are employees second. When they come to work, they expect their technology to work like it works in their homes or in their cars. They also expect to be treated the way they are treated in other commercial establishments—as customers with economic value.

In a recent conversation, Frank Slootman, the chief executive officer (CEO) of ServiceNow, reminded me that CIOs can play key roles in improving and elevating the work environment at their companies. As many of you already know, ServiceNow is the enterprise cloud company providing a service model that defines, structures, and automates the flow of work, removing e-mail and spreadsheets from the process to streamline the delivery of services.

"The enterprise needs to catch up with the consumer service experience," says Frank. "When we go home at night, we're dealing with Amazon, Google, and other online sites providing world-class service. We bring those expectations from home to work, and we expect our service experience in the workplace to match our service experience at home."

But when employees experience problems with technology and they have to wait in a phone queue or physically stand in line to have their devices checked, that's when IT gets a bad rap. "The enterprise service experience needs to improve, and the CIO should provide the tools to make it happen," says Frank.

IT has become the backbone for almost every business process, which means that every stakeholder is impacted by the quality of IT service. Great CIOs make sure that service quality remains high, even when IT is under pressure to reduce costs. "Some CIOs are so focused with controlling costs that they don't see the harm they're doing by allowing service quality to decline. But it's almost always a mistake that comes back to haunt you."

Frank sees a giant opportunity for IT to deliver real value to the enterprise by mastering the processes and technologies required to manage data from the Internet of Things. "The Internet of Things will be huge. Every device—from medical scanners to cars to printers to refrigerators—will have an IP address and will be managed through the IT backbone. When everything is programmable and connected, the standard notions of IT management will evolve greatly," says Frank.

I really appreciate Frank's candor and vision. He outlines a brilliant future for CIOs who are willing to embrace the realities of the modern service culture and bring it into the twenty-first-century global enterprise.

Leaders Leverage the Interplay between Consumer and Business Technologies

Ten years ago, it was common for CIOs to dismiss the influence of consumer technology on the enterprise. Today, it's hard to find a CIO who isn't deeply aware of trends in consumer technology. When I speak with CIOs, I find a general sense of agreement that, sooner or later, trends in consumer technology become trends in the enterprise.

Roger Gurnani is executive vice president (EVP) and CIO at Verizon, where he has a unique view of the current trends in consumer and business technology. Like most CIOs, Roger understands the interplay between consumer tech and enterprise IT. He also sees that interplay from the perspective of a seasoned corporate executive.

"Mobile devices are increasingly becoming smart devices, giving consumers access to an incredibly wide range of information," says Roger. "Because of their increased access to information, consumers are far more knowledgeable than ever before. They expect and they demand more transparency."

Since people who work in corporations are also consumers, they tend to expect greater transparency from their corporate employers. "All of this has huge implications for IT," notes Roger. "New IT systems, new IT architectures, and new philosophies for providing IT services must accommodate those shifting expectations."

Businesses are also changing the ways in which they interact with their customers, since most business customers are also users of consumer technology. "We're seeing a fundamental shift in the way that businesses connect and engage with their customers," says Roger.

The rapid transformation of technology also means that IT has to do a better job of communicating and engaging with the company's business leaders. At Verizon, Roger makes sure that every senior executive in the business has an IT leader responsible for providing the IT services required by that executive to achieve his or her business objectives. Those "one-to-one" relationships between the business executives and IT leaders have become an essential part of IT strategy.

Additionally, Roger works hard to make sure that IT leaders genuinely understand the needs of the business units they are supporting. As a result of that deep understanding, planning cycles can be closely aligned and integrated for maximum effectiveness. "The value of IT can be more fully realized when everyone—whether they're in sales, marketing, operations, or IT—is aiming for the same goal," says Roger.

I really admire how Roger clearly sees the big picture and appreciates how all the various pieces of the enterprise fit together to create a seamless entity. I have to believe that Verizon's collaborative approach and aligned strategies account for a large part of the company's continuing success in a highly competitive market.

CIO Leadership Must Move beyond the Boundaries of Traditional IT

I recently had an excellent conversation with Mike Benson, the EVP and CIO at DIRECTV. Mike is considered a true executive leader, and he has assembled a top-notch IT team that enables DIRECTV to compete successfully in rapidly changing markets. I asked him to describe the traits that he looks when hiring an IT leader.

"As IT evolves, we will be pushed further and further out into the enterprise. As a result of that outward push, IT will become less monolithic and more focused on helping the business," says Mike. "We spend a lot of time discussing the kinds of skills and talents that we need to make a smooth transition from being an organization focused on process to becoming an organization focused on customer experiences."

I really like how Mike sets up the challenge of finding the right people for the twenty-first-century IT shop. From Mike's perspective, good IT leaders possess a blend of technology, business, and emotional skills. "I look for people who can be IT leaders and leaders in the business," says Mike. "From my viewpoint, the best person is someone who can do a good job within the IT organization and also step outside of the IT organization to work directly with the business."

A case in point: In 2012, DIRECTV decided to improve many of its customer-facing processes, essentially making them easier for customers to use. The company looked long and hard to find the right leaders for the project. Eventually, an IT executive was picked to lead the initiative. In addition to technical skills, the IT executive had business experience and was highly trusted by other executives across the enterprise.

"We knew that he would go a great job of collaborating with executives from sales, marketing, operations, and all of the groups whose support was necessary to make the initiative a success," says Mike.

I love this story because it illustrates how IT can help the enterprise overcome challenges that are not purely technical in nature. The choice of an IT executive to lead an important enterprise-wide initiative clearly demonstrates that Mike's team is ready to tackle any assignment.

"IT sees the whole enterprise and all of its various parts," says Mike. "We have a unique perspective that enables us to help the company achieve its goals and objectives. We can also mend bridges where there have been challenges and facilitate collaboration among the various parts of the enterprise."

Mike genuinely embodies the principles of modern IT leadership, and it is always a pleasure speaking with him.

Great CIOs Learn the Business's Needs and Use IT to Drive Success across the Enterprise

I had a truly excellent conversation with Ramón Baez, SVP and CIO at HP. I have known Ramón for many years, and it is always a great pleasure speaking with him and listening to his stories. I'm also glad that he agreed to write the Foreword for this book!

When I asked Ramón about his approach to IT leadership, he told me that he relies on a straightforward strategy with three basic components: operational excellence, innovation, and talent management.

"Some CIOs tend to overlook the importance of talent management," says Ramón. "But it's a critical part of your role as an executive leader. You need to strike a balance between nurturing your 'legacy' talent and bringing new talent on board. Achieving that balance can be difficult. You want to send the right message to the IT organization and you also want to hire people with fantastic skills. Essentially, you have to do both."

Building talent, he says, requires two intertwined disciplines: training existing employees and acquiring new employees with new skills. "You need a blend of experienced people and new people. You need fresh eyes, but you can't look outside the company for every new hire. You also need to grow the skills of the people within the IT organization."

In addition to focusing on talent, Ramón says that he's also spending lots of time meeting directly with HP customers. "I currently spend about 20 percent of my time meeting with external customers," says Ramón. He estimates that the amount of time he spends with external customers will roughly double in the months ahead. "Our customers like to see the CIO in sales meetings because it sends a strong message of confidence in our products and services."

Ramón also says that he spends a significant portion of his time meeting with the company's business leaders and learning about their operations. I genuinely believe that Ramón's willingness to see IT from the perspective of the business units—in other words, his ability to put himself in someone else's shoes—is a critical factor in his success as a senior executive. Whether you call it business acumen or business empathy, Ramón has an uncanny ability to perceive the needs of the business, and to deliver IT solutions that effectively address those needs.

One of the key lessons that I have learned from Ramón is that successful CIOs take the time to understand the financials of the business units. The very best CIOs listen carefully to how the business units define success in finance terms, and then make sure that IT strategy is aligned to support those goals.

Chapter 4

Exceptional Leadership

EXECUTIVE SUMMARY

In virtually every business scenario, leadership makes the critical difference between success and failure. Great CIOs take the time to understand the facets of leadership and to develop the interpersonal skills necessary for inspiring high-performance teams over the long term.

There are many truly excellent presentations at our CIO Executive Leadership Summits. We are genuinely honored by the depth and relevancy of the speakers and their topics. Not all of our speakers and presenters are IT executives—but each of them is interesting in a unique way.

Eric McNulty is director of Research and Professional Programs and Program Faculty at the National Preparedness Leadership Initiative (NPLI), a joint program of the Harvard School of Public Health and the Center for Public Leadership at Harvard's Kennedy School of Government. He is also an instructor at the Harvard School of Public Health. At one of our summits last year, Eric spoke passionately about the need for CIOs to develop real crisis leadership skills proactively. Why proactively? Because, as Eric notes, the best time to learn the ABCs of crisis leadership is *before* a crisis strikes. Since we seem to be living in a period of perpetual crisis, Eric's advice seems at first like common sense. But it's the kind of common sense that many top executives ignore until it's too late.

"Crisis management and crisis leadership are not the same thing," says Eric. "When a crisis occurs, 70 percent of your energy is dedicated to managing it. But the remaining 30 percent should be dedicated to leading through it. In a crisis, leadership is about the human factors. You have to understand how you personally function when you're under stress, how your team functions, and other stakeholders such as suppliers and customers."

The most common mistake made by executives is the failure to understand their own personalities. "You need to reset your brain after the shock of the crisis and avoid the temptation to focus exclusively on operational details," says Eric. "Leaders must remember to lead and not get lost in the weeds. You have to grasp the big picture as well as the details."

Experienced executives know that minor crises happen regularly and that a small crisis can provide a great training opportunity. "You can actually practice your crisis skills during a small crisis," says Eric. "You can also run drills and exercises that will prepare your teams for handling a large crisis when it arises. A little preparation can really make a big difference."

Remember that a large crisis will extend beyond the traditional boundaries of your organization. A serious crisis will engulf your teams, your organization, and your extended supply chain. "In a real crisis, you will be required to supply a lot of leadership, which is why it's a good idea to develop the skills and resiliency needed for crisis leadership now, before the crisis occurs."

Begin by assuming that everyone on the team needs to be part of the solution. "People tend to think that leadership is about individual skills, but it's really more about group skills," says Eric. "Great leaders catalyze other people, they connect key stakeholders, they embrace complexity, and they don't get stuck in the weeds. They also accept that some things are beyond their control, and they focus on the reality at hand to shape the best possible outcome."

Eric offers some excellent advice for all of us in executive posts. Crises are inevitable, and when they strike, people look for real leaders to guide them. As CIOs and IT executives, we are perfectly positioned to pitch in and offer the kind of calm, practical leadership that is required in a crisis.

Great CIOs Leverage Trust and Deep Knowledge to Provide Real Business Value in Rapidly Changing Times

"The more things change, the more they remain the same." Jean-Baptiste Alphonse Karr, a French journalist and novelist, made that famous observation back in the nineteenth century. It was true then, and it remains true now. Karr's observation seems especially relevant when we look at the changing nature of the CIO's role as an executive leader in the modern global enterprise.

As the pace of innovation quickens, the enterprise naturally looks to the CIO for guidance and advice in a range of areas beyond pure technology. Increasingly, the CIO is cast in the role of trusted advisor, counselor and transformational leader. The CIO is expected to enable business process transformation, advise the board on critical infrastructure investments, and offer mature perspectives on new technologies.

In a time of rapid change and uncertainty, the CIO should be an island of stability and tranquility, a rock of sound judgment, and a reliable source of clear-eyed wisdom. From my perspective, the CIO is uniquely positioned to offer the kind of solid, trustworthy advice that growing companies need. Unlike other corporate executives, the CIO has the ability to see across the multiple lines and functions of the enterprise. IT is pervasive and ubiquitous, creating a lens through which the CIO can observe the innermost workings of the enterprise from a neutral position.

Great CIOs leverage their knowledge and wisdom to build strong bridges across the C-suite. They work hard to understand the corporate strategy, provide meaningful results, and deliver real business value.

Great CIOs understand the following:

- Global and local economies are experiencing an unprecedented cycle of rapid change and innovation.
- CIOs are the only C-suite executives with unobstructed views across the enterprise and its multiple functional areas.
- CIOs must deliver tangible business value.

- CIOs must actively engage in driving, leading, and enabling initiatives around cloud, mobile, social, and analytics.

- The role of the CIO is continuously evolving.

- The enterprise expects the CIO to provide sound, trustworthy, and timely counsel on the intersection of technology and business.

As I've said and written before, now is a great time to be the CIO. Enjoy the moment, and keep building those bridges across the C-suite.

Great CIOs and IT Vendors Work Together on Long-Term Strategy

IT is a complex blend of people, processes, and technologies. Because of its inherent complexity and often-vast scale, there's a very real temptation to approach IT piecemeal—in bits, chunks, or easily manageable portions.

The problem with a piecemeal approach is that it makes it awfully difficult to follow through on a comprehensive IT strategy. Tactics are great, but you need a successful strategy to make a difference over the long run.

After meeting with hundreds of CIOs and senior IT executives, I am convinced that the genuinely transformational leaders are the ones who focus on strategy over tactics. Tactics can help you win battles, but they won't help you win the war.

Ironically, I see similar patterns of behavior among IT vendors. Some focus on short-term wins that make their sales teams look good, but don't really move the ball forward for their customers. Vendors who focus exclusively on tactical victories often miss opportunities for big sales. And from what I've seen, they are usually the first ones edged out when the market softens and demand tapers off.

Strategic vendors, however, keep their eye on the big picture. In my experience, I've seen strategic vendors stay the course and maintain important relationships with their customers, even in bad times. It usually takes longer for strategic vendors to close deals, but they tend to be more profitable since they focus on nurturing long-term relationships that generate significant amounts of revenue over time.

The net takeaway here is that CIOs and IT vendors have good economic incentives for taking the long view and resisting the urge to settle for quick victories that might look good on paper but don't contribute meaningfully to the bottom line.

What's needed now is a thorough and in-depth discussion of IT strategy and the long-term IT value proposition. The discussion should include all of the stakeholders in the process. That means that CIOs have to elevate their game and do a much better job of explaining the IT value proposition to the C-suite.

CIOs should focus on building deeper relationships with their C-suite colleagues and raising levels of trust. Building better relationships between IT and the C-suite should be considered a fundamental part of the CIO's strategy for long-term success.

The alternative is allowing decisions to be made piecemeal, at the business unit level. That's a scenario that can lead to poor outcomes for both IT and the enterprise. It's far better to wrap the decision-making process into a high-level strategy, which will assure a coherent and cost-effective approach to IT investment over the long term.

A piecemeal approach to IT might provide some temporary relief, but it won't help the company win a larger share of its market or raise its earnings over time.

Great leaders focus on strategy, and then select tactics that support their strategy. That's the right way to run a successful business organization.

Keep IT Relevant to the Business in Modern Dynamic Markets

There's no question that information technology is on the rise. But the expectations have also changed dramatically. For some CIOs, moving from an *execution focus* to a *partnership focus* can be a major challenge. The shift in emphasis from *technology transformation* to *business transformation* can also be problematic.

The best way to surmount those challenges and excel as an IT leader is by keeping yourself—and the IT organization—supremely relevant to the rest of the enterprise.

The critical importance of staying relevant to the business emerged as a key takeaway at a recent Financial Services CIO Executive Leadership Summit at the Harvard Club in New York.

Several speakers and panelists echoed the idea of relevancy throughout the event, which attracted world-class CIOs and IT leaders from across the New York Metropolitan area. There was a general sense of agreement that IT leadership has evolved beyond reducing costs and increasing efficiencies. Today's corporate boards want CIOs who can pitch in and drive value across the enterprise. They want CIOs who understand markets and are ready to deliver practical technology solutions that truly enable business growth.

Boards also want CIOs who can attract top talent and create work environments that support teamwork, innovation, and meaningful collaboration. Moreover, corporate boards put a premium on CIOs who can communicate clearly, aren't afraid to speak up, and are prepared to take advantage of business opportunities when they arise.

I was impressed by the sense of purpose among the CIOs at the summit. They seem ready and eager to embrace new challenges and to assume greater responsibilities as full-fledged members of the C-suite. The atmosphere was extremely positive, constructive, and confident. Those are good signs, and they bode well for the future of CIOs in the modern enterprise.

There was also talk of rebranding IT and appealing to younger people who want to work with cutting-edge technologies. I think that's a great idea, and it will go a long way toward helping CIOs become magnets for top talent. Several CIOs said they feel confident about competing with Silicon Valley for top talent in dynamic markets, which is excellent news.

I was also intrigued by a lively discussion about the need for rebalancing the ratio of contractors to in-house employees in many IT organizations. Conversations like that clearly demonstrate that IT is perceived as a driver of value, and not just a commodity that can be easily outsourced.

I left the summit with a heightened sense of optimism, energy, and enthusiasm for the rising potential of IT leadership. I genuinely feel that the tide is turning, and that we are entering a new "golden era" for CIOs and IT organizations.

Use Best Practices for Building Bridges across the C-Suite

Since graduating from the US Military Academy in 1980, Clif Triplett has worked in seven different industries, including automotive, aerospace, energy, and telecommunications. His varied experiences have definitely shaped his approach to IT leadership and have consistently enabled him to find innovative solutions to complex challenges over a career spanning more than three decades.

Today, Clif is managing partner at SteelPointe Partners, LLP, a global management consulting, professional services, and outsourcing firm based in Texas. I caught up with Clif recently and asked him to share his "best practices" for

building bridges across the C-suite and communicating effectively with other C-level executives. "I talk to them in business
terms, not in technical terms. I say, 'Look, our quality is taking
a hit because of this particular issue,' or, 'Our increased work-
flow has caused a bottleneck here,' or, 'We need to upgrade
this technology to solve a particular business problem.' I try
to give them the whole picture, and explain what's happening
from the perspective of people, process, and technology."

Clif advises CIOs to use their "unique vision" across the
enterprise to offer constructive ideas that will help their companies achieve their business goals. "The CIO is the only
person who gets to see how the whole company works.
You need to take advantage of that perspective and speak
up when you see opportunities for improvement."

For Clif, the idea of perspective is critical. The ability to look
around you and find solutions from available resources is an
essential part of his executive playbook. "That's what innovation is all about—applying something you learned from one
circumstance to another. When I hire people, I look for maximum diversity. I look for people with experience in different
industries, different countries, and different cultures. I believe
that the more diversity you have, the more likely you are to
find the answers you need to solve problems."

I asked Clif why some CIOs can't seem to reach out to their
colleagues across the enterprise and partner effectively with
other executives.

"Part of it has to do with the historic role of the CIO as an order-taker, a person who waits for someone else to ask for something instead of speaking up and being proactive," says Clif. "If someone says, 'We need a cloud service,' for example, try to steer the conversation back to the business outcome. Find out what's really going on, and then work collaboratively to find a solution to the business problem."

A former US Army officer, Clif hates the idea of "just sitting around and waiting for someone to tell you what to do." Great CIOs offer suggestions, provide solutions, and deliver on their promises. "You have to define your own job," says Clif. "Take ownership and take responsibility."

Clif also offered some great advice on crisis leadership, a topic that we're hearing more about these days. "Practice on the small stuff, so when the big problem arises, everyone knows their role and knows exactly what they need to do. Don't wait for the crisis. Practice for it every day. Build confidence in the recovery process. Then when something major occurs, people will be calm, they will respond quickly, and you'll be able to deal with the crisis effectively."

From Clif's vantage point, the key to success as a CIO is leadership. "The technology hasn't changed as much as most people think. The typical problems you face as an executive leader are basically the same as they've always been. When you're explaining something, you need to tell the story from the perspective of the audience. Understand their motivation and use their language. It's okay to build on the story, but keep the changes simple. Always explain the logic in business terms."

Will CIOs Experience Similar Career Trajectories as CFOs?

A recent conversation with Gregory Roberts of Accenture inspired a fascinating question: What if CIOs and CFOs had similar career trajectories?

Greg is a managing director in Accenture's Communications, Media and Technology practice. In our conversation, he mentioned the similarities he sees in the evolution of the CFO and CIO roles.

"Back in the [19]80s and '90s, the CFO role was very much internally focused. If you look at CFOs today, they're very externally focused. They are tight to the market and tight to their shareholders," he notes. "In many cases, it's the VP of Finance who handles the inward-facing operational duties."

From Greg's perspective, the CIO's role is evolving into an outward-facing executive with executive leadership skills and a keen sense of the market. "I think the CIO's future is very much taking the same path as the CFO," says Greg. "The most successful CIOs are externally facing executives who talk directly with the folks in the business. In the high-tech space, CIOs often work directly with the company's external customers as well."

Greg sees the CIO's evolution as part of the overall shift in focus from inward-facing processes to outward-facing processes. "CIOs need to realize there's been a shift in expectations," says Greg. "CEOs, CFOs, and COOs assume that e-mail and other basic IT systems will work. They are looking for CIOs who can bring together technology and business processes to create value."

Problems tend to surface when the CIO doesn't step forward or fails to act as a true partner to the business. That's when *shadow IT* emerges. Greg and I agree that great CIOs are willing to assume the responsibilities of executive leadership, even when those responsibilities take them out of their comfort zone. For example, today's CIOs need to understand the benefits of high-performance analytics from a business perspective. They also need to make sure they've have access to the infrastructure required to run high-performance analytics and deliver real value to the business.

"Historically, CIOs were able to accomplish their responsibilities within the four walls of the IT department. Outsourcing changed that mindset, but only to a certain degree," notes Greg. "Today, the great CIOs take a partnering approach. They understand that they might not have the expertise necessary to accomplish everything they need to do, and they look for partners who can help them. That reflects an evolving maturity that wasn't always there in the past."

Greg suggests that great CIOs of the future will act as brokers who are capable of working with a wide variety of partners. "I do think it's going to be interesting to see that evolution over time," says Greg.

The modern enterprise puts a high value on growth and operational efficiency. IT needs to deliver on those expectations. Great CIOs provide the leadership necessary to meet future business needs with speed, transparency, and accountability. If there's one thing we all surely agree on, it's that IT cannot become an impediment to value creation.

Advanced analytics, machine learning, and the Internet of Things are three areas where CIOs must provide credible leadership and make absolutely certain that IT is aligned with the business.

Greg and his colleagues at Accenture have articulated eight essential capabilities that IT must deliver to the business:

1. *Strategic agility.* Sense and respond quickly to industry shifts.

2. *Innovation.* Constantly identify and create new sources of value.

3. *Adaptability.* Collaborate and integrate easily across markets, firms, and functions.

4. *Differentiation.* Sustain and grow competitive advantage.

5. *Speed to market.* Deliver new capabilities quickly, and at scale.

6. *Flexibility.* Architect business processes and applications to be fluid and adaptive.

7. *Optimization.* Reduce technical debt and operational complexities.

8. *Transparency.* Ensure clear visibility into value economics across functions.

Is your IT organization prepared to partner with the business, and are you ready to deliver on those expectations?

I personally believe that CIOs will step up and assume their roles as true partners with the business. If they don't, they will open the door to competition from other executives within the enterprise.

The future of IT is exceptionally bright, and the potential for success is unlimited. The enterprise is counting on us to deliver the expertise, processes, and technologies required to get the job done. I am confident that we will.

When Building Tighter Relationships with the C-Suite, Location Matters

I've written a lot in the past five years about the importance of building stronger working relationships between the CIO and the rest of the C-suite. In many instances, it's far easier to build relationships when your office is located near another group of executives.

As any real estate agent will tell you, location matters. It's no different when you're talking about building trust at the C-level of a corporation. Location matters. The more closely located your office is to, say, the CEO and the CFO, the more often you are likely to bump into them by chance—and oftentimes those random, unplanned meetings are great opportunities to exchange ideas and stay up-to-date on what's going on in other parts of the enterprise.

I thought about the value of co-located offices while reading an article by my friend Peter High.[1] Peter's main topic was how Google CIO Ben Fried is redefining the role of IT at what is surely one of the world's most innovative technology companies.

Peter wrote about Fried's bold mission of providing Google employees (aka *Googlers*) with world-leading technology, and Peter noted how strongly Fried believes in the value of developing tight collaborative relationships with the company's other functional units. Working closely with other Googlers enables IT to grasp problems more intuitively. As a result, IT becomes quicker at providing practical tools and solutions.

Here's a passage from Peter's article that really struck me as significant:

Like other executives, Fried also encourages his team to think of their workspaces as fluid. Individuals tend not to have fixed spaces, but rather gather in clusters that are emblematic of the collaborations that are necessary given a topic or project that is under way. On the day that I visited Fried's New York office, members of the IT team occupied office space with members of the product law department based on project ideas that required the expertise of each, as an example.

I think that Peter's observation is genuinely useful to all of us who are striving to create better relationships across the enterprise. I'm sure that we all know CIOs who spend incredible amounts of time traveling to far-flung regions of the world for the purpose of meeting personally with IT employees. There's nothing wrong with that practice, and in many cases, it's unavoidable. After all, we are living in a global economy, and making sure that everyone is on the same page often requires face-to-face meetings.

But I am also certain that many CIOs could build better, tighter, and more trusting relationships at the corporate headquarters by making sure their office is located near the offices of the other C-level executives.

It might sound like a no-brainer, but location still matters. Video conferencing is a great tool, and getting better all the time. But nothing beats sitting down and having lunch with a colleague. Sometimes those informal meetings are the best opportunities for building trust and developing an intuitive sense of what the business needs.

Delivering Real Business Value from Technology Investments

I caught up with my good friend Tim Stanley recently, and we had a truly excellent and highly energizing conversation. Tim is a brilliant consultant, and the former senior vice president of Enterprise Strategy + Cloud Innovation at Salesforce.com. Previously, Tim was the chief innovation officer, CIO/CTO,

and senior vice president of innovation, gaming, and technology for Caesars/Harrah's Entertainment, where he was
responsible for many of the award-winning innovations and
initiatives that enabled the company to grow into the largest
casino, hospitality, and entertainment company in the world.

Tim's deep experience makes him a uniquely qualified
source of critical information, and I asked him for his
perspectives on the evolving role of the CIO as a key player
on the C-suite executive team. He offered three great nuggets
of advice:

"One, you've got to be in the game. Sure, I understand
that CIOs tend to resist change, but you've got to gain some
first-hand familiarity with way the consumers see things. You
need to get your hands dirty and your feet wet," says Tim.
"If you don't, you're either going to get run over or wind up
being just a naysayer."

"Two, you need to develop a symbiotic relationship with
the CMO. Maybe you'll even help with the CMO's hiring process or you'll create a hybrid model where you'll staff teams
together. CIOs typically don't get involved with marketing
agencies on the creative side, but when the CMO is working
with a digital agency, you'll want to be involved and know
what's going on, because sooner or later they're going to need
data from the IT team," says Tim.

"Three, you need to understand how some of the new
social media and web 2.0 platforms are being co-opted for the
enterprise. I'm seeing the re-emergence of corporate intranets

and extranets. I think there's a big opportunity for CIOs to emerge as de facto thought leaders for marketing projects that require a real understanding of how collaboration technologies and mobile platforms work, for internal customers and partners, and for external suppliers and distributors. This is going to be really big, and the CIO needs to provide both expertise and leadership to the enterprise."

I really love Tim's vision of the highly involved, hands-on CIO who leads by example, partners with the business, and shares incredibly valuable insight across the enterprise. And I agree with Tim that newer mobile and collaboration technologies will require the expertise and experience of seasoned CIOs and senior IT leaders to deliver real value.

At one point in our conversation, Tim estimated that most CIOs have about two-thirds of the knowledge required to lead the enterprise through the next phases of technology evolution. That means we need to start learning even faster, or risk falling behind the curve.

As a group, I believe that CIOs are ready to embrace the challenge. What do you think?

Transforming Vendor Relationships from Transactional to Strategic

Managing vendors is a top priority for CIOs. When your job is providing essential IT services to the business, great relationships with key suppliers are absolutely critical. That's why I'm always interested in hearing about CIOs who excel at vendor management. I want to share what I learned from Ken Piddington, the former CIO of Global Partners LP.

Here's some background on the company: Global Partners is a leader in the logistics of transporting Bakken and Canadian crude oil and other energy products via rail, establishing a "virtual pipeline" from the mid-continent region of the United States and Canada to refiners and other customers on the East and West Coasts.

Global owns, controls, or has access to one of the largest terminal networks of petroleum products and renewable fuels in the Northeast, and is one of the largest wholesale distributors of gasoline, distillates, residual oil, and renewable fuels in New England and New York. With a portfolio of approximately 1,000 locations in nine states, Global is also one of the largest independent owners, suppliers, and operators of gasoline stations and convenience stores in the Northeast. Global Partners is No. 157 in the Fortune 500 list of America's largest corporations, and trades on the New York Stock Exchange under the ticker symbol GLP.

Ken himself is a leader in the area of vendor management, and I asked him to tell me about the company's highly innovative Strategic Partner Program.

"When I became CIO, I looked closely at our IT portfolio. I discovered many vendors providing services that no longer matched our needs. In many cases, the dollars just didn't make sense," Ken recalls. All of the vendors, it seemed, were in full sales mode, but "we weren't having real conversations about the value they would bring to our company. We knew that we needed a new set of ground rules. There had to be a better way."

Ken's solution was the Strategic Partner Program. "It was specifically a partner initiative, rather than a vendor initiative. We knew where our company needed to go, and we knew we would need good partners to get there. We decided to engage with our partners differently than we had in the past. We would be more open, and in return, they would provide much more value to us."

Instead of explaining the new concept in traditional one-on-one meetings, Ken hosted a Partner Summit for 60-plus vendors. "We hosted a dinner for about 120 people. We shared the history of our company and laid out the ground rules for partnering with us. We told them what we would expect from them and what they could expect from us."

The program has been running for almost four years, and the results are impressive. "It's led to much higher value for the dollars spent, higher quality of services, fewer shiny boxes off the shelf, and more real solutions," says Ken. "At the annual summits, we give out awards to the vendors who go above and beyond. They see the tangible benefits of partnering with us."

The program also includes a vendor showcase and a vendor education component. "We continue to evolve the program and add more components," Ken explains. "It really makes a world of difference."

I genuinely believe the program Ken devised is truly brilliant. It moved the company's relationships with its vendors out of the transactional sales mode and into the strategic partnership mode. As IT continues to expand its role as a driver of value across the enterprise, those kinds of strategic relationships become more than just incredibly valuable—they become real competitive advantages in rapidly changing markets.

In EMEA, Demand Rises for Two Types of CIOs

In September 2014, HMG Strategy held the CIO Executive Leadership Summit in London. It was a great success, and vastly increased the scale and quality of our IT leadership network in Europe. Not long after the London summit, I asked Kevin Sealy about the challenges and opportunities facing CIOs in EMEA (Europe, the Middle East, and Africa).

Kevin is a senior client partner in Korn Ferry's London office, where he leads the firm's Information Technology Officers Center of Expertise in EMEA. He has 30 years of experience in the IT industry, and has worked with many leading companies on high-profile chief information officer–related placements.

"There's high demand here for two different flavors of CIO," says Kevin. "There's still a strong demand for CIOs who can drive global operating models for IT efficiency. And of course there's a fast-growing need for CIOs who understand how to harness newer digital technologies and consumer IT."

The first type of CIO is required by global companies that have grown through mergers and acquisitions. As a result, those companies tend to have multiple legacy IT environments, and are seeking a CIO with the leadership skills required to drive standardization and cost efficiency across the enterprise. "In a global economy, large companies need to respond quickly to changes in their markets, and simplifying the IT environment enables them to respond at speed," says Kevin.

The second type of CIO is sought by companies that need to ramp up their digital capabilities to not only provide better marketing, sales, and customer service but also facilitate new ways of working right the way across the life cycle. "Those CIOs must be highly technical literate. They've got to really understand the newer technologies and understand how those technologies can be leveraged to improve the customer experience," says Kevin. "They've got to be very proactive and ready to bring ideas to the table."

In the past, says Kevin, chief executives would often say they wanted a CIO who can define an IT strategy that supports the business strategy. Today, chief executives look for CIOs who enable strategy and who play a proactive role in developing strategy and bringing new ideas into play based on their technology insight. That shift places much heavier burdens on the CIO, but it also opens doors for CIOs who are willing to accept new challenges and serve as genuine leaders at the CXO level.

I find it absolutely fascinating that many companies still look for CIOs with the experience and leadership skills to drive standardization, but then again, perhaps it is not that surprising, given the increasing need for agility and speed within globally dispersed and highly decentralized corporations and the requirement for IT to remove complexity. I also find it fascinating that many companies are looking for CIOs who can reorient their IT organizations to accommodate the expectations of today's digitally empowered consumers. To succeed, both types of CIOs will need superior leadership skills and consummate technical knowledge.

Forecast: Trends Point to Growth for Visionary CIOs and IT Leaders

Looking ahead, the potential for CIOs and IT leaders to achieve higher levels of success seems virtually unlimited. I am extremely optimistic, and here's why:

- The combination of social, mobile, cloud, and big data are creating new demands from the business for more IT services. The business wants everything faster, better, and bigger—and naturally looks to the CIO to get the job done.

- The Internet of Things, the Industrial Internet, the Internet of Everything—no matter what you call it, it's a game-changer!

- The war for talent puts new emphasis on the CIO's ability to find, recruit, hire, and retain top performers. Great CIOs will become "talent magnets" to attract the best people and build the best teams.

- Rising demand from the business translates into more clout for CIOs seeking budget increases to upgrade infrastructure, hire more staff, and provide more services.

Looking at the trends, I foresee a long period of healthy growth for IT. Thanks to the ubiquity of information technology, CIOs have unparalleled vision into every corner and crevice of the modern enterprise. This unique and extraordinary perspective creates amazing leverage that smart CIOs will use to their advantage.

In the near future, we will see the rapid spread and wider adoption of newer technologies such as 3D printing, additive manufacturing, geospatial marketing, mobile medicine, and wearable computers. All of the newer technologies will depend on IT to make them practical engines of business growth.

As I've written before, successful CIOs combine leadership, innovation, and transformation to drive real value across the enterprise and support the strategic goals of the business. I am highly confident that higher demand for business-critical IT services will result in higher profiles, increased strategic relevancy, and greater success for CIOs and IT leaders in 2015 and beyond.

Note

1. Peter High, "Google IT's Mission to Empower Googlers with World Leading Technology," *Forbes* (July 22, 2013), http://www.forbes.com/sites/peterhigh/2013/07/22 /google-its-mission-to-empower-googlers-with-world -leading-technology/

Chapter 5

How Much, How Fast?

EXECUTIVE SUMMARY

We all understand that technology is a key component in continuous innovation and business growth, but the incredibly rapid acceleration of technological evolution often makes it hard to determine which platform or which vendor is the best fit. CIOs need to develop their own strategies for staying in front of technological change and making choices based on what's logical over the long term for their companies.

When I began writing *On Top of the Cloud* in 2011,[1] many CIOs were still trying to determine if the cloud was a fad, a trend, or a genuine transformation. I think that most of us can agree that the cloud represents genuine change, but the nature and extent of that change is still up for debate.

Two years ago, many people assumed that when others mentioned the cloud, they were referring to some kind of public cloud service. Today, most IT executives have a much more nuanced view of the cloud. They understand that the cloud can assume many shapes and forms.

For example, I frequently hear CIOs talking about the cloud as a kind of virtual mechanism for helping them manage intense bursts of activity or temporary overflows. I also hear CIOs talking more about their plans to build private clouds. Many are working with vendors or consultants to develop hybrid public/private cloud solutions.

Far from being "the end of IT as we know it," the cloud seems to be finding its place among the other essential components of the enterprise technology portfolio. People are beginning to realize that the cloud is more complementary than revolutionary. When you need it, the cloud can be very helpful. When you don't need it, the cloud seems almost invisible.

I can remember when some pundits predicted that cloud computing would make IT unnecessary. They were wrong, of course. The IT team is still responsible for most of the same tasks that it's been doing for the past several decades. The main difference is that some of those tasks and responsibilities now take place in the cloud. As a result, some tasks have become easier to manage and others have become slightly more cumbersome to manage since it can be harder to tell precisely where certain IT operations occur in the cloud.

For many routine operations, location isn't an issue. But in some regulated industries—such as financial services, health-care, and pharma—you don't have the freedom to send your data into the cloud. Data storage and data processing can get especially complicated in Europe, where privacy controls are generally more restrictive than in the United States.

The idea that the cloud would somehow render corporate IT departments irrelevant or obsolete is simply not true. The cloud has simplified IT operations in some ways, and made them more complicated in other ways. Like all new technologies, the cloud is still evolving. The journey is far from over, and there's a long road ahead of us.

It's also important to remember that the cloud is only one of several new technologies that are having a huge impact on all of us. In addition to dealing with the challenges and opportunities of cloud computing, we are also dealing with social, mobile, and big data. Each of those new technologies comes with a different set of unknowns.

Today's CIO has a full plate of critical tasks and important responsibilities. Leveraging the potential of the cloud and integrating cloud capabilities into the existing IT portfolio are just a couple of the action items on a long list of chores.

Create a Smart Process for Engaging Successfully with SaaS Providers

I had an exceptionally valuable conversation recently with Gerri Martin-Flickinger, the CIO at Adobe. Gerri and I share several beliefs about the role of the CIO and the ongoing relevancy of IT in globally networked markets. In her excellent post "How to Capitalize on the Golden Age of IT Innovation", Gerri writes that IT has reached "an inflection point ... where the conversation is moving from cost to value. IT is no longer focused on back-office infrastructure ... the IT function plays an integral role in delivering delightful customer experiences across all digital platforms."[2]

I truly believe that Gerri captures the essence of the "big shift" concept, in which IT evolves from an inward-looking to an outward-looking business function. The old boundaries are disappearing; new relationships between IT and the rest of the world are emerging.

Gerri's worldview has an immediately practical side. Like all great CIOs, she understands intuitively that new ideas must be translated into processes that people can easily follow. For example, Adobe has created a process for business units that want to use cloud-based services. It's called the "SaaS Toolkit for Business Units," and it includes a list of best practices for engaging with SaaS providers.

In addition to detailing a step-by-step process for purchasing a SaaS solution, it clearly spells out the goals of a software as a service (SaaS) deployment. Here's my quick paraphrase of the goals listed in the toolkit:

- Always protect the company's data and systems.
- Check in with the IT Business Services Team for support (e.g., integration requirements, operational processes).
- Eliminate unnecessary redundant third-party SaaS provider purchases.
- Obtain service-level agreements (SLAs) for all new third-party SaaS providers.
- Purchase all third-party SaaS solutions through procurement.
- Procurement and legal should negotiate the best SaaS contract and SLA terms.
- Ensure that the company has control of its data when decommissioning a SaaS provider.
- Eliminate legal risks.

The process outlined in the toolkit includes steps such as defining and documenting business requirements; working with the IT team; sourcing the best SaaS providers; reviewing security and architecture for potential issues; and working with the company's procurement team.

I genuinely admire the immensely practical way in which Adobe has created a smart process for managing SaaS purchases by business units. From my perspective, Gerri and her team are great role models for IT leaders who want to partner with the business, drive growth, and create value.

Great CIOs Know When They Have Hit the Limits of IT Outsourcing

We've all hear and read a lot about outsourcing IT. At first glance, the economies of outsourcing almost seem too good to be true. A deeper look reveals all kinds of potential problems, headaches, and invisible costs.

That doesn't mean that outsourcing is all bad—it means there are limits to how much you can outsource IT before the risks begin to outweigh the benefits.

What you want to avoid, says Dave Smoley, is transforming the IT department into an organization of service managers. Dave is a good friend and a valued advisor. He is also the CIO at AstraZeneca, a global biopharmaceutical company that spans the entire value chain of medicine—from discovery, to early- and late-stage development to manufacturing and distribution, and finally to the global commercialization of primary care, specialty care–led, and specialty care medicines.

Before joining AstraZeneca, Dave was senior vice president and CIO of Flextronics International. Previously, Dave held senior posts at Honeywell and General Electric, where he was director and CIO for GE Power Controls in Barcelona.

Dave is incredibly thoughtful, and I find his view on outsourcing exceptionally valuable. "You can't allow IT to become a bureaucracy where people manage people who manage vendors," says Dave.

Let's say, for example, that you need to develop a specialized application that requires the skills of eight separate vendors. Every time you want to upgrade or modify the application, you'll need to coordinate the efforts of those eight vendors. That's a sure sign that you've hit the limits of IT outsourcing.

Granting too high a level of decision-making power to vendors is an "abdication of responsibility," says Dave.

None of that, however, means that Dave is against cloud-based SaaS models. "The cloud and mobile are enabling a new kind of shift in which IT moves away from its focus on heavy infrastructure and refocuses on providing capabilities to the business. With the cloud and mobile, you can scale up and scale down much faster when you need to solve a business problem."

Dave says that decisions regarding the cloud are based on five values:

1. Customer focus
2. Technical leadership

3. Operational excellence

4. Simplification

5. Collaboration

"We work within the broader culture of AstraZeneca, where we put the patient first and we follow the science," Dave explains. "We're building an IT team that asks questions such as, 'What's right for the customer?' 'What does the customer need?' 'Are we adding value?' 'Have we picked the right best technology?' and 'Are we on top of managing it?'"

From Dave's perspective, the fifth bullet on his list of values—collaboration—is potentially the most critical. "Almost everything we do now has to be done across company boundaries and across different departments. For us, collaboration is the key to our success," says Dave.

Dave's understanding of the new IT leadership paradigm is truly impressive, and I'm delighted that he took the time to share his thoughts with us.

Building Trust in the Enterprise Requires Focus, Energy, and Great Leadership

Patty Hatter was already the senior vice president of operations when she was appointed CIO at McAfee, the world's largest dedicated security technology company.

One of her primary tasks as CIO was restoring the IT department's credibility as a trusted partner across the enterprise. "The trust between IT and every other business function had broken, and we had to correct that quickly," she told us recently. Patty, who holds both master's and bachelor's degrees in mechanical engineering from Carnegie-Mellon University, took a scientific approach to the task.

"We had to work quickly, so we focused on three areas: transparency, IT organization stabilization, and effective execution. Those became our three main objectives. By focusing on these, we rebuilt trust by communicating and delivering on our commitments to business units; and by default, we built leadership and teamwork within our IT organization," she said.

Patty's experience as head of operations helped her rebuild IT's relationships at the executive level. She also worked diligently to make IT more transparent to the rest of the enterprise. "Transparency is really the key to building better relationships. If someone wanted to talk with me about the IT budget, I would spend time going through the budget and explaining the details. Spending extra time to explain details to someone can be an effective way to raise the level of trust," she said. "People want to know that when they ask you questions, they're getting truthful answers."

Patty also had to stabilize the workforce within the IT organization. "We had to pull together the team, raise morale, and bring attrition down to manageable levels," she said. Modifying IT's organizational structure also helped. For example, the number of vice presidents was reduced from six to three. "Reorganizing IT caused some pain, but it resulted in much better leadership. Today, our people in IT have someone to go to when they have a problem and they know that somebody has their back," said Patty.

Patty's third objective was driving better execution. "Don't try to be fancy, and don't try to second guess other people," said Patty. "Just concentrate on demonstrating to the other business functions that IT is a credible partner and that we can really get things done. Establishing your credibility as a trustworthy partner enables you to focus on the next wave of exciting new technology," said Patty.

"We're able to be much more proactive now. The people on the team feel good about themselves. There's a trusting relationship between IT and the rest of the company," said Patty. "People believe that when they bring in IT, we'll get the job done."

Patty's determination and leadership have proven invaluable as she leads the McAfee IT and Operations integration with Intel throughout 2015. "Establishing ourselves as a true business partner at the forefront of security technology and delivering innovative business solutions has positioned us well within the greater Intel organization," she said.

I genuinely appreciate Patty's candor and willingness to share her three-part methodology. I love listening to stories about successful turnarounds, especially when they involve great IT leadership.

Use the CenterPoint to Maintain Alignment, Adapt to Change, and Sustain Execution

I've had the honor and privilege of working recently with John Foley, who is truly one of the world's most inspiring motivational speakers. As many of you know, John is a former US Navy Blue Angels pilot. His experiences on that genuinely awesome precision flying team are an essential part of his presentations, and they offer many relevant lessons for modern CIOs.

The CenterPoint™ is a Blue Angels concept that is especially relevant for CIOs and IT leaders. From John's perspective, every organization needs a CenterPoint—it's a "north star" that everyone in the organization recognizes and understands. High-performance organizations use CenterPoints to maintain alignment, adapt to change, and sustain execution at peak levels.

"Not all CenterPoints are created equal," John explains. "You can have tactical CenterPoints and strategic center points. The Blue Angels have tactical CenterPoints we use for reference while flying air shows (a building when we're flying over land, a boat when we're flying over water) and a strategic CenterPoint that defines our larger purpose—we're the US Navy's ambassadors of goodwill."

During his presentations, John describes how the Blue Angels use the CenterPoint concept in their amazing air shows. "One of our most exciting maneuvers is the Loop Break Cross, in which we all zoom off in different directions. From the audience's viewpoint, it looks like we've disappeared. Moments later, we reappear in a 'stack'—each plane crossing over the same point, but at different altitudes," says John.

The "secret" of the stack is this: Before every air show, the Blue Angels identify an object on the ground or in the water that's easy to see from the air. "It becomes our common focal point, and each of us knows exactly where it is. No matter what kind of maneuver we're flying, we use it as a reference to keep us aligned," John explains.

The CenterPoint is a valuable tool for CIOs and IT leaders who need to maintain alignment and focus over the course of long and complicated projects. If you can establish a CenterPoint—a common point of reference that everyone can easily grasp—you're much more likely to achieve your goals, on time and on budget. It's also extremely useful for maintaining critical alignment between the CIO, the C-suite, and multiple business units of the enterprise.

Nobody expects the IT organization to perform ultra-precise aerial maneuvers like the Loop Break Cross. But we can still learn from the experiences of great teams like the Blue Angels, who establish a common CenterPoint and always know exactly where to find it.

Does your IT organization have a CenterPoint? I think it's a great idea that's definitely worth trying.

Build Deep Foundations of Trust with Simple Contracts

Watching John's presentations is a little bit like flying with the Blue Angels. You really feel inspired! In addition to the cool flying videos, he also talks about trust. I've written extensively about how successful CIOs extend their influence by building bridges to the C-suite. John reminded me that CIOs also need to focus on inspiring deep trust—not only across the C-suite and the IT organization but throughout the enterprise.

How do you inspire trust in a global enterprise? As with most undertakings, it's always best to start small. By "small," I don't mean something that's unimportant or trivial—I mean something that can be accomplished and replicated until it becomes a solid foundation for something bigger. Here's one of John's stories that illustrates my point. It's about the Knife-Edge Pass, one of the most dramatic aerial maneuvers flown by the Blue Angels:

"Air show audiences love the Knife-Edge Pass," says John. "Here's how we do it: The two solo pilots line up at opposite ends of the field and then fly right towards each other at 500 miles per hour. At the last possible moment, both pilots roll their jets 90 degrees and narrowly avoid a head-on collision. You pass within a wingspan of the other plane. Sometimes you're so close that you feel a 'thump' as the airflow changes. The audience always gasps."

Executing the maneuver requires some great piloting skills. But as John explains, "the secret to flying the maneuver successfully is trust. That trust is sealed with a contract between me and my wingman."

The contract between John and his wingman is short and sweet: "I'll miss you." That's it—a simple, direct statement that carries a whole lot of weight. Simple, unadorned contracts like that are foundational to the success of high-performance teams like the Blue Angels.

Nobody expects the IT organization to perform ultra-precise aerial maneuvers like the Knife-Edge Pass, but we can still learn from experiences of great teams like the Blue Angels, who build their incredible performances on solid foundations of deep trust.

True Leaders Embrace the Challenge and Accept the Risk

It feels as though we're at another inflection point in the history of IT leadership. So much of the world around us is changing so quickly that sometimes it feels easier to "lead from behind" than to get out in front.

For the CIO, however, adopting a pose of passivity would be a strategic mistake. True leadership requires a blend of vision, courage, and endurance. Now is the time for leadership, pure and simple. Yes, you still have to figure out a way to hedge your bets, but that doesn't give you a free pass to sit out the revolution.

Make no mistake. The technology revolution hasn't stopped—it hasn't even paused! Every day brings word of newer technologies that get the job done better, faster, and cheaper than before. Moore's law has not been repealed—it remains in full force, and it continues to impact every aspect of technology development.

The intertwined and interconnected evolution of cloud, social, and mobile technologies is still in the early stages. From where I stand, it looks like we're still in the opening innings of a long and interesting game.

Meanwhile, the CIO's executive responsibilities are also growing. CIOs must continue building strong relationships across the C-suite, communicating clearly and honestly with stakeholders across the enterprise, maintaining partnerships with business units, improving operations while driving down costs, and planning for investment in new infrastructure.

In many ways, it feels like we're all strapped onto the same rocket, streaking upward into the stratosphere. It might be a bumpy ride, but the risks are worth taking.

In the past, the "burning platform" was often the technology. We needed to make the leap from mainframes to client-servers to PCs to mobile, and so on. Today, the burning platform is leadership. We need to build a platform for genuine leadership, a platform that will empower and enable us to lead IT with honesty, integrity, openness, and transparency. We'll need to jettison or subdue some of the traits that brought us to the CIO role and adopt new ways of looking at the world.

In addition to our traditional roles as caretakers and corporate stewards, we also need to step forward and lead the revolution. Our experience, our insight, and our knowledge of technology is extremely valuable in a turbulent and growing global economy.

There is absolutely no sign that the technology revolution is slowing down—in fact, it is accelerating. As IT leaders, we possess the skills and the wisdom to leverage that revolution and convert its massive energy into an engine of growth and continuous value creation.

As I've written before, now is the best time to be an IT leader. Make sure that you enjoy it, and always remember that real leaders get out in front, embrace the challenges, and accept the risks. Active leadership is not only a winning strategy—it's really the only kind of leadership that works.

Notes

1. Hunter Muller, *On Top of the Cloud: How CIOs Leverage New Technologies to Drive Change and Build Value Across the Enterprise* (Hoboken, NJ: John Wiley & Sons, 2012).

2. Geri Martin-Flickinger, "How to Capitalize on the Golden Age of IT Innovation," LinkedIn.com, July 22, 2014, https://www.linkedin.com/pulse/20140722223122 -1798994-how-to-capitalize-on-the-golden-age-of-it -innovation?trk=prof-post.

Chapter 6

Security, Big Data, and the Internet of Things

EXECUTIVE SUMMARY

The convergence of big data, super-efficient networks, social media, inexpensive sensors, and a new generation of advanced analytics has created an enormous range of opportunities for businesses to grow by entering new markets or leveraging operational efficiencies in existing markets. Those opportunities, however, are accompanied by serious risks. Cybercrime has emerged as a major concern for CIOs, who are increasingly being held responsible for protecting the enterprise from the consequences of cybercrime.

I had an excellent conversation last week with two friends in the executive search business. We covered a wide range of interesting subjects, but one topic we discussed stayed at the front of my mind. The topic was cybersecurity and the chief information officer (CIO).

Until relatively recently, the CIO could safely delegate cybersecurity responsibilities to a variety of other corporate executives, including the CISO (chief information security officer) and the CRO (chief risk officer). In some organizations, cybersecurity was handled by the CFO. Many CIOs simply delegated cybersecurity oversight to members of the IT staff.

The days when the CIO could deflect or sidestep responsibility for cybersecurity are over, according to my friends in executive search. The main reason for the shift in attitude is that executive boards are now held accountable when cybersecurity breaches occur. Today, board members rightfully worry about liability and reputational damage stemming from cyber attacks.

When the board is concerned about an area of potential liability, it makes sense to prepare for a session of tough questions. My advice is to start preparing now for your conversation with the board about cybersecurity.

Board members don't live in a vacuum, and they are well aware that cyber attacks are on the rise, both in terms of frequency and severity. A recent report from the World Economic Forum, prepared in collaboration with McKinsey & Company, paints a grim picture of cybersecurity risks and the consequences of cyber attacks.[1]

According to the report, some CIOs and CISOs "estimate that indirect or unaccounted security requirements drive as much as 20–30% of overall technology spending, crowding other projects that could create business value."

This part of the report is especially noteworthy: "Current trends could result in a backlash against digitization, with huge economic impact. Major technology trends like massive analytics, cloud computing and big data could create between US$9.6 trillion and US$21.6 trillion in value for the global economy. If attacker sophistication outpaces defender capabilities—resulting in more destructive attacks—a wave of new regulations and corporate policies could slow innovation, with an aggregate economic impact of around US$3 trillion."[2]

In other words, some organizations will feel obligated to spend so much money on cybersecurity that they will have to sacrifice making investments in key technologies such as cloud, analytics, and big data. If that trend materializes, it would slow down the progress of technology innovation significantly.

You Can't Build a Wall High Enough to Keep out the Bad Guys

Recently, I've had the good fortune of spending quality time with Israel Martinez, a globally recognized expert in board-level strategies that minimize the balance-sheet impact and individual liability of cyber compromises. He is chairman of Axon Global and National Partner, Global Cyber Practice, Technology Strategy, and Innovation at the prestigious Newport Board Group.

He is also the author of the proprietary playbook, *What Every CEO Should Know Before, During and After a Cyber Attack.* He is a recognized leader in enterprise risk management, cybersecurity, cyber counter intelligence, and digital identity.

I have learned a lot from my conversations with him. For example, most of us typically tend to think of strategy in terms of "defense" and "offense." But when it comes to cybersecurity, our laws and traditions make it very difficult to pursue genuinely "offensive" strategies against cyber criminals. So we need to take a more nuanced approach, and look more closely at our security strategies. There are passive strategies, such as the infamous Maginot Line, which involves erecting barriers, securing defensive perimeters, and hoping the enemy won't merely go around them or work from the inside.

There are also what Israel calls *offensive security* strategies, which require a deeper understanding of how the bad guys operate, better knowledge of the threat environment, more readiness, and continual awareness.

"You can't build a wall that's high enough," he says. "The bad guys are very sophisticated, and they move much faster than the good guys. That's the reality of the world we live in."

The biggest challenge, he says, is becoming desensitized to the risks. For some executives, it's easier to ignore the problem than to deal with it. Sooner or later, however, that approach will result in a major breach. "You have to presume that you will be compromised tomorrow," says Israel.

That doesn't mean throwing in the towel. It means you need to prepare. You need to train your staff, make them aware of the danger, and teach them to recognize the signs of an impending cyber attack.

Resist the urge to play the "blame game," says Israel, because that merely encourages a culture of denial. "Train, train, train," he recommends.

Sooner or later, all of us are likely to experience some kind of cyber attack. Will you be prepared, and will you know how to respond when it happens?

Leveraging Data across the Enterprise

My good friend Stephen Gold is the senior vice president and chief information officer for CVS Health. I asked Steve recently about the shift to consumer-centric IT and its impact on large retailers. Steve shared some valuable insights.

"Most companies don't manage their data assets in a strategic way that creates real business value. Data are fragmented by area of the business, and each area is responsible for managing their own data," Steve says. "Great companies, on the other hand, understand the value of their data. They elevate their data *platforms to the same level of their* systems *platforms. They administer and manage their data assets strategically, across multiple lines of business, in ways that are parallel and complementary. In this way, they truly leverage their data and create new value from it."*

Steve says this is all especially relevant in the healthcare space. Consumer empowerment is transforming many delivery models. Steve says, "As you are aware, the rise of consumer-directed healthcare plans puts more responsibility and accountability into the hands of the consumer. Modern consumers are accustomed to shopping and communicating online, in real time. Our goal is offering similar tools to consumers in the healthcare environment."

"Until recently, most of the healthcare environment was like The Wizard of Oz, *in which Dorothy is told, 'Pay no attention to the man behind the curtain.' Today, consumers have a front row seat. They want more information, more choice and less friction. From my perspective, companies that provide tools and capabilities for connecting all of the participants in the healthcare delivery system will be the market leaders of tomorrow."*

Steve offered a compelling example from the healthcare space that illustrates the value of a strategic approach to managing data: "Let's say a patient takes medication that requires prior authorization from a doctor. Here's the way it works today: The patient either brings the prescription to a pharmacy, or if the doctor has electronic prescribing capability, the prescription is electronically transmitted to the pharmacy. Either way, the patient must show up at the pharmacy to pick up the prescription."

But here's a common scenario, Steve says. "Sometimes the patient arrives at the pharmacy before the doctor's authorization is received. The pharmacist tells the patient, 'You can't have this medication without prior authorization from your doctor.' The patient leaves without the medication, the pharmacist tries to call the doctor, they play phone tag for three days, the patient calls the pharmacy, maybe the patient goes back to the pharmacy, but the pharmacist can't fill the prescription without authorization from the doctor. It's a very fragmented process."

CVS Health is developing systems in which the required authorizations are transmitted electronically, in real time. Steve says, "Our goal is taking the friction out of the process—and creating positive experiences for our customers."

I genuinely appreciate how Steve explains the value of integrated enterprise data strategies from the perspective of both the business and its customers. For me, Steve's insights really capture the spirit and impact of the big shift in IT from an inward-facing department of systems to an outward-facing integrated service function that drives value to the business.

The New Water Cooler for Better Decisions

Here's a theme I've been hearing recently from forward-thinking CIOs: The C-suite wants better tools for visualizing data. From my perspective, that makes total sense. We've been hearing about the value of big data for several years, but less has been said about the optimal ways for consuming the insights generated from big data.

It's impossible for most people to figure out what's going on by just looking at a spreadsheet or a huge set of data points. Most of us—me included—need to look at some kind of graphic representation, whether it's a pie chart or a bar graph, before we appreciate the value of data.

Good data visualization tools are essential for understanding data and appreciating its value. My colleagues at HMG Strategy recently spoke with Lee Feinberg, a data visualization expert, to get a clearer picture of how smart organizations get the most from their data. Lee is president and founder of DecisionViz, a management consultancy that helps companies become great communicators of data and build leadership around the most challenging aspects of data visualization. DecisionViz developed the Blue Ocean for Visualization™ Framework to accelerate adoption of visualization and analytics in a practical, repeatable approach.

Lee says, "The mindset about data visualization is changing. In the past, most people thought of it as an activity, like making charts or creating dashboards. Today, people are beginning to understand that data visualization is a

strategic function. Data have strategic value, and data visu-
alization is part of a strategic process."

Some organizations try to solve the problem by buying
new technology. Lee says, "That's a step, but it doesn't
solve the problem. You also have to make organizational
changes. You need to understand how your organization
uses data. The technology part is easier. Making the
technology effective is the harder part. You need to get the
people and processes right. You need to understand your
organization's strengths and weaknesses, and then you
need to build a plan that accelerates the adoption of data
analytics and visualization throughout the organization."

Lee further explains, "As human beings, we are wired
to process images. We're not so good at processing rows
and columns of numbers." Lee says that data visualization
enables IT leaders to work with data in three important
ways:

1. Exploration. *That's looking for patterns in the data.*
   Trends and patterns are clearer when you're looking
   at visual representations of data, as opposed to looking
   at numbers on a spreadsheet.

2. Communication. *Data visualization is becoming a*
   medium for communications within the organiza-
   tion. Lee says, "It's a way of distributing insights that
   other people can absorb quickly." Think of it as the
   new "water cooler" for quickly sharing information
   among groups, especially among decision makers.

3. Data sharing. *Sharing data with customers is a*
   growing trend in healthcare, and will likely spread to

other areas, including finance and travel. Customers can interact with your data through simple visuals on their laptops, smart phones, or mobile devices.

Lee says, "My advice to companies is simple: Don't focus exclusively on the technology. If you're just focusing on the technology and you don't look at the broader perspective of people, process, and cultural change, you'll miss opportunities to truly transform your business."

We asked Lee what CIOs should know about using data visualization to create value in the enterprise and how they can provide leadership to the C-suite when questions about data visualization arise:

Visualization makes data much more accessible to more people than ever before. The impact of that is now you've got more people who are actually more knowledgeable about the company. They can understand what's going on. When they're more knowledgeable, they make better decisions.

When people have the ability to interpret data more easily and make better decisions, the feedback loop gets faster. You have the data, you understand the data, you take action, and you're able to improve outcomes faster.

Now you're really changing the dynamics of how the company works. Some people might be uncomfortable with that. It depends on the culture of the organization. 'Data democratization,' the idea of more people having access to data, is really about "decision democratization." Data visualization empowers more people in the company to make decisions. For many companies, it will require a genuinely big shift. It won't happen overnight. There will be organizational challenges.

But the time to start thinking about this is now. You need to start training people in the organization so they have the skills to handle data and make data-driven decisions. For some companies, data visualization will be disruptive. You also need to begin hiring people who can function in a world that's driven by data. By the way, people who enter the workforce today want to participate, communicate and make decisions. Not every company is ready for that.

We also asked Lee to explain the difference between business intelligence (BI) and big data analytics. "When most people hear BI, they think of something like operational reporting, which is where somebody (probably from IT) sets up a bunch of reports and then they just run them forever. They generate information about what's happening in the business. Then you can either access them over the web or you get them in your email. Users don't have much of a way to interact with them. They can't really tailor them. It's more of a 'set it and forget it' model."

Lee says, "I prefer to look at BI differently. I see BI as a process that helps people understand the business better, drives decision making, and makes it easier to take action. To me, BI encompasses many skills and domains of knowledge, not just reporting."

"Advanced analytics is something very different. With advanced or predictive analytics, you're taking data and trying to estimate who might buy a certain product or who

might respond to an ad or who's at risk for canceling your service. This is different from operation reporting because you are trying to discover patterns and relationships in the data. Very often today, this is what people are talking about with respect to big data analytics."

The good news is that analytic software has been simplified. It's now easier for the average person to use. However, that will likely disrupt some companies, since it means more people will be using analytics. "Even with simpler software, you will still need people who understand statistics so they can interpret what the software is telling them. They don't necessarily have to be data scientists, but they'll need to understand the basics of statistical analysis. Depending on the scenario, they'll need to know how algorithms work because you need algorithms to sift through data and analyze it. The bottom line is that you'll have to teach people how to swim before you throw them into the lake. Or you can hire people who already know how to swim."

Additionally, we asked Lee to describe what make a great BI dashboard. Here's a summary of his reply: "For me, a dashboard includes a set of visuals that communicates a message very simply. If you try to put too much information on a dashboard, you're defeating its purpose. Limit the screen to four visuals, at most; I really prefer three. Your brain doesn't really assimilate more than four things at a time anyway and you don't want your dashboard to be visually distracting.

"If you make the dashboard confusing or difficult to read, people will ignore it. The goal is making it easy for people to

absorb the information. It sounds obvious, but you need to follow best practices. There's been lots of research over the years about how we process visual information. Our brains process some kinds of information faster than other kinds of information. You have to respect the brain's hierarchy when you're designing data visualizations."

As a final question, we asked Lee to describe what he sees over the horizon for the data visualization industry: "Mobile is a new frontier for analytics. We're seeing companies investing in capabilities for consuming and creating information on mobile devices. Mobile is gaining traction because executives prefer seeing information on their smart phones and tablets. The executives are driving the migration to mobile because it's what they want."

Lee says, "Another area of growth is search-based analytics. It's still under the radar for most people, but in the near future, you won't start an analysis by firing up software and plugging in data. Instead, you'll type or say a search phrase, such as 'sales revenue eastern region third quarter 2015,' and the information will come up on the screen of whatever device you're using, in a format that's optimized for the display on that device."

I'm delighted that Lee took the time and energy to talk us through an important subject. As I mentioned at the beginning of this section, I'm hearing more CIOs talking about enhancing or improving their data visualization capabilities. It's also interesting that some CIOs are making an effort to get ahead of the curve on data visualization, and not waiting for a grassroots, bottoms-up movement to catch them unprepared. To me, that seems like the right approach.

As Markets Evolve, IT Focus Shifts to Business Results

I had a great conversation a few weeks ago with Doug Harr, the CIO of Splunk, one of the genuine leaders in real-time operational intelligence for the modern enterprise. More than 7,000 enterprises, government agencies, universities, and service providers in over 90 countries use Splunk software to deepen business and customer understanding, mitigate cyber-security risk, prevent fraud, improve service performance, and reduce cost.

Back in the early days of big data, real-time analytics were seen mostly as tools for increasing efficiency and driving down costs. While those benefits are still an important part of the overall value prop, more companies are beginning to see the strategic business value of real-time big data analytics.

"In the beginning, it was all about cost savings and running infrastructure effectively," Doug explains. "Then companies began looking at big data to improve security. And then the focus shifted to using big data for understanding customers better and engaging with them more effectively, giving business real insight into their digital assets."

As companies began to look at big data more creatively, new business models arose. It was the beginning of an exciting new cycle of business innovation that's still going strong.

When IT leaders hear the term *big data,* they tend to think of Hadoop. Interestingly, Splunk was founded at roughly the same time that Hadoop emerged as a big data platform. Like Hadoop, they are optimized around the three Vs of big data (volume, velocity, and variety), but Splunk is more oriented toward real-time data analysis. In other words, Splunk is all about real-time insights and results, which makes it a good fit for business users.

"We originally approached big data from the IT operations front," says Doug. "Our product was developed by operations experts who'd worked at Disney and Apple—very large corporations with huge data centers. As a result, we have the ability to forward the data in from its many points of origin, manage that data based on time, and provide search and analytics access via a role-based security model. We're very much a commercial-grade tool set that's vertically integrated, with a robust security model."

From my perspective, the story of Splunk's success is part of the big shift that I've been writing about in previous chapters. The shift, as I describe it, is from inward-facing technology solutions to outward-facing technology strategies. Past generations of IT leaders focused on meeting the needs of internal customers. Today's IT leaders respond to the demands of the company's *real* customers—the paying customers who purchase the company's good and services. Great companies don't merely satisfy their customers, they delight them!

IT is now part of every smart company's go-to-market strategy. Savvy IT leaders know that their job is delighting customers, which is the best way to grow the company's top line. IT will always play an important role in managing costs and improving the bottom line, but the days when IT was seen as nothing more than an efficiency platform are over.

In today's hyper-competitive global economy, IT is truly indispensable. The evolution and success of software companies such as Splunk highlights the path we're on for the foreseeable future. As I've written before, the big shift is more than a trend—it's a roadmap for the evolving and deepening relationship between IT and the business.

Hadoop and the Enterprise Data Warehouse

If you're a CIO or senior IT leader, I'm sure you've already heard some variant of this question from a C-suite executive: "Why can't we replace our costly enterprise data warehouse with a less expensive Hadoop cluster?"

As IT people, we understand that Hadoop is not a replacement for the data warehouse. Hadoop can augment and add capability to some data-related services that IT provides, but I don't know any company that is about to ditch its data warehouse and replace it with Hadoop.

Some will argue that Hadoop is more economical because it's based on open source code. Maybe the underlying code is free, but the rest of what you will need to convert your data into actionable business information is going to cost real money. There are some great reasons why enterprise data warehouses provided by vendors such as Oracle, Microsoft,

IBM, and Teradata are still popular. Those older systems still work just fine, and there's no shortage of people with the skills to run them.

As usual, it's not just a matter of migrating to a new kind of technology. You also have to hire the talent and develop the processes that will enable your new technology to deliver real business value. Where big data is concerned, there is no "one-stop shopping" or "one-size-fits-all" solution.

Quite a lot of the newer technology requires a healthy dose of DIY (do it yourself). That's okay if you've got the time, energy, and interest to get down into the weeds and write code on weekends. If you're working against a deadline, dealing with highly valuable transactional information, or handling confidential customer data, then those old-fashioned enterprise data warehouses offer exactly the kind of safety, security, and reliability that you need to the job done.

That said, there is still an important role for Hadoop in the enterprise. Hadoop is perfect for handling huge loads of "messy" public data that don't correspond neatly with the schema of traditional database management systems. If you need to analyze terabytes of data from sensors and web logs, then a Hadoop cluster is probably a wise investment.

Based on my research, it seems clear that smart CIOs will find a place for Hadoop within the enterprise IT portfolio—not as a replacement for the data warehouse, but as an additional resource that enables more agility and greater flexibility. There's no question that we need faster, smarter, and more powerful data analytics. The real challenge is finding the appropriate balance between traditional and newer technologies.

It's not a matter of Hadoop *or* the enterprise data warehouse. The right solution probably includes both.

Great CIOs Perceive the Opportunities and Benefits of Consumer IT in the Enterprise

Much has been said and written about the consumerization of IT and its potentially harmful impact on enterprise IT. Since it seems highly unlikely that consumer IT will disappear anytime soon, I think it makes more sense to talk about the ways in which consumer IT can complement and augment enterprise IT.

My friend Steve Phillips has a refreshingly pragmatic perspective on the "enterprise vs. consumer" debate. Steve is the senior vice president and CIO at Avnet, one of the world's largest distributors of electronic components, computer products, and embedded technologies, serving more than 100,000 customers in more than 120 countries. From Steve's point of view, a major role of IT is helping the company leverage technology to achieve its business goals. In most instances, traditional enterprise IT is the right tool for getting the job done. But in some instances, the right tool might be a consumer technology product such as a smartphone or a tablet.

"I don't see consumer IT and enterprise IT as contradictory," says Steve. "The consumerization of IT offers great opportunities and benefits to companies, especially in terms of end user device choice. While we need to be careful around information security and delineating between personal data and enterprise information, I don't see a conflict between enterprise IT and consumer IT. Achieving your business goal is what's important, and many consumer tools and devices are now mainstream in the enterprise."

I respect Steve's willingness and ability to see both sides of the debate. On one hand, enterprise IT will almost always be the safer choice in terms of security and reliability. On the other hand, people are comfortable with consumer tools and will use them readily. When speed is essential, going with a familiar tool is probably the right choice. When security is the first consideration, it makes sense to rely on proven enterprise technology.

"It's a challenge for IT leaders, but as our focus shifts more from technology to business, we need to embrace the challenge, become fully engaged, and help the organization make the transition," says Steve.

In a way, the evolution of the CIO reflects the previous evolution of the CFO, whose initial responsibilities were tightly focused on a narrow set of specialized finance skills. Over time, the CFO's role broadened and became considerably more strategic.

"A lot of good CIOs have made that transition and become full partners of the business," says Steve. "We're responsible for IT, but we're business leaders as much as we're technology leaders."

When you look at the CIO's role from that perspective, it seems logical to view the consumerization of IT as an asset, rather than as a liability. When everyone brings their own device to work, it makes sense to create an environment where those devices can be used safely and securely. Far from being a threat, consumer technologies can provide smart CIOs with opportunities to prove the value of IT to the business.

Connected Devices Are Smarter and Smaller

Andi Mann is VP of Strategic Solutions at CA Technologies and an expert across cloud, mainframe, midrange, server, and desktop systems. Andi is a brilliant guy and extremely knowledgeable. I spoke recently with him about a wide of topics, ranging from the "Internet of Cars" to smart cameras.

"We've all heard or read about the Internet of Things. But what excites me more is the Internet of Cars. Automakers are placing sensors in their cars, and those sensors will enable a car to communicate in real time with other cars on the road. The upshot is that everyone driving has a better picture of what's going on ahead of them in terms of traffic, weather, and road conditions. That kind of communication is fantastic, and it speaks to the value of IT in all of our lives," says Andi.

Andi is also interested in the newest generation of wearable technologies, and recently picked up a Garmin VIRB "action camera," which is a digital camera equipped with Wi-Fi and a high-sensitivity GPS. "I took it on a ski trip. It actually tracks you all over the mountain. You wear it and it tracks your speed and acceleration," Andi says. "I've paired it with a sensor for my heartbeat to make sure I'm not having a heart attack. It has a big button, so it's easy to operate – even when you're wearing ski gloves. It's wonderful!"

From Andi's perspective as an IT professional, devices like that are much more than toys; they represent the next big wave of technology. "Sure, I'm a bit of a data geek, but the point is that here's a device that's highly functional, use-specific, and wearable. That's what the future of IT looks like."

Although noting that the small size of some wearable devices might limit their utility, Andi is still quite optimistic about their growing impact on business.

"We're not at the point where we can pack a full size computer into the form of a watch or a camera or a FitBit. You have to be selective about what you do. The one thing I have seen is the idea of wearables playing a role in mobile finance. Think about these watches: They're too small to do general purpose computing, but plenty big enough to do mobile payments or interact with loyalty programs. For example, at the Disney Resorts, you can make payments using a wristband. I think that sort of thing is going to be very interesting across a variety of business scenarios."

I really love how Andi's mind grasps how smarter and smaller technologies have the potential to fundamentally alter the IT universe. It's fair to say that we've moved beyond the "consumerization of IT" stage and we are entering a new era in which transformational technologies can emerge from almost anywhere. It's an exciting time to be in the IT industry, and the next generation of "smart devices"—whether they're cars, cameras or thermostats—will have a significant impact on all of us.

Transforming IT Is a Critical Step in Building Strong Relationships with the Business

It would be great if we could start every new job with a clean slate, but that's not usually how it works in the real world. When Rob Lux was named SVP and CIO at Freddie Mac in 2010, the relationships between IT and the company's business divisions was, he says, suboptimal. Rob knew that one of the first items on his agenda would be repairing and rebuilding these essential relationships.

"IT was split into separate groups reporting to different people," says Rob. This led to coordination issues, stalled or delayed big projects, and, ultimately, a general lack of confidence in the IT function.

Moving in the right direction meant consolidating IT under the CIO's leadership. "In the past, when something went wrong, no one knew who was in charge. Now, if there's a problem with IT, everyone knows that I'm responsible," he says.

Rob also made sure that IT had a strategic plan. "Previous programs to transform Freddie Mac's technology had failed. I realized that before we could transform the technology, we had to transform IT," says Rob. "We had to transform ourselves into a capable, competent organization that delivers on its promises."

Under Rob's leadership, IT focused on four main areas of improvement. "First, we needed to improve our ability to plan. Second, we needed the ability to deliver projects on time, on budget, and with the original intended scope as quickly as possible. Third, we needed to focus on operations. We were really good at operations before I got here, but it cost too much. We had to simplify the operational footprint while maintaining the uptime levels people had come to expect," Rob explains.

"Fourth and most important, we focused on building our IT team. That meant bringing in some outside hires who had experiences at other organizations. But we also had lots of great talent here that we elevated into positions of leadership," says Rob.

The results of Rob's efforts are genuinely admirable. In his blog, he writes that "it only took Freddie Mac 17 business days to write, test, and deploy the 100+ rule changes comprising our Hurricane Sandy disaster relief policies for the systems lenders use to sell and service Freddie Mac mortgages. That is about 90 percent less time than it took to operationalize policy changes following disasters like Hurricane Katrina or the 2012 New England floods."

Prior to its transformation, IT had normally required 18 months to complete a typical project and begin delivering value to the business. Today, 30 percent of Freddie Mac's IT projects are developed with Agile methodology and 75 percent of its projects are delivered in six months or less, Rob says.

From my perspective, Rob's accomplishments as an IT leader are truly exemplary. Best of all, the transformation of IT has resulted in a much stronger and significantly more positive relationship between IT and the business. That's great news for everybody, at every level and in every part of the enterprise.

Create a Process and a Platform for Change and Innovation in the Modern Enterprise

Several months ago I had a great conversation with Cynthia Stoddard, senior vice president and CIO at NetApp. Our conversation focused on the role of IT as an agent of change in the modern enterprise, and the stories that Cindy shared are especially valuable for IT leaders at all levels.

First some background: NetApp creates innovative technology products that help customers store, manage, protect, and retain their data. A Fortune 500 company with $6.3 billion in annual revenue, NetApp has been included on Fortune's "100 Best" list for 12 consecutive years.

Under Cindy's leadership, IT has evolved from a largely invisible back-office function into a trusted partner that drives business innovation. It's important to make the distinction between "innovation for the sake of innovation" and innovation that creates real business value. Cindy and her colleagues at NetApp focus on delivering innovation that solves real-world business problems.

"We want IT to help the business move forward," explains Cindy. "But you cannot innovate in a vacuum. You have to understand the needs of the business, and everyone in the IT organization should be involved and making a contribution."

To emphasize the idea that innovation can arise from any part of the IT department, IT was rebranded "IT One Team." Five general principles were drafted to set the stage for a culture of continuous innovation:

1. Appoint the *right leader* to lead a small team.

2. Establish a *framework* for innovation.

3. Demonstrate *incremental wins,* with business value achieved.

4. Provide consistent and visible executive *leadership*.

5. Gain respect, acknowledgment, and funding—through *success.*

I genuinely admire how Cindy and her team created a process and a discipline around the concept of innovation. Lots of companies talk in generalities about innovation, but NetApp has taken specific steps to create a sturdy platform that leverages the expertise of IT and supports innovation as an ongoing process for generating business value.

Here's a great story that Cindy shared with me: Since NetApp has employees, partners, and customers all over the globe, it's often difficult to schedule conference calls. Sometimes people in the United States would schedule calls for Friday afternoon, which meant that it was already Saturday morning in many parts of the world. An innovative solution emerged from one of the IT groups: No conference calls after 12 P.M. on Fridays. "It might seem simple, but it's had a big impact on the organization in terms of time management and reduced stress," says Cindy.

Clearly, there are benefits to creating a culture of innovation. When great ideas surface—even when they don't come from R&D—there's a good chance they will be considered, evaluated, and tested. In my experience, companies that create a fast lane for great ideas are more likely to gain winning advantages in the market.

Worried about UI versus UX? Focus Instead on Delivering Great CX

I attended recently an interesting meeting of the Society for Information Management (SIM) in Manhattan. The meeting was hosted by Microsoft, and naturally there was some discussion of Microsoft's ongoing transformation from a software company to a devices company. One of the presenters spoke about how Microsoft is shifting its focus from the UI (user interface) to the UX (user experience), which makes sense within the broader context of the company's strategic goals.

As I was driving home, I thought about the UI versus UX dichotomy. It seems to me that an ideal device would have a user interface that consistently delivers a great user experience. I don't see the problem as "UI *versus* UX." It's not a competition or a zero-sum game. From my perspective, the real question is, how do you design a device in which the UI enables the best-possible UX?

To many people, terms like UI and UX still sound too much like engineering jargon. It would be better if we replaced *user experience* with *customer experience*. That brings us closer to the real goals of the business, which are achieving the highest possible levels of customer satisfaction, customer loyalty, and lifetime customer value. Those are the goals that make the cash register ring. Achieving those goals drives revenue and growth.

Using the term *customer experience* (CX) reminds us that no products or devices exist in a vacuum. Without paying customers, it doesn't matter how cool your product's UI looks. At best, the UI is a means to an end—a tactic, not a strategy.

Why is this discussion relevant for CIOs and IT leaders? I think it's relevant because we are increasingly asked to think like the customer. We are asked to extend our imaginations beyond the traditional firewall and visualize how the solutions we provide will look and feel to the company's external customers. That's a big change from the way we operated 15 or 20 years ago. But it's a change for the better.

For the past decade, we've been talking about the critical importance of aligning IT with the business. I think that many CIOs are moving their IT organizations in the right direction and are subtly shifting the emphasis from pure operational excellence to a mix of operational excellence and customer satisfaction. Great CIOs reject the either/or scenario. Instead, they seek a nuanced blend of qualities that result in consistently superior results for the business.

For the business, it's all about the customer experience. If the UI doesn't deliver great CX, it's back to the drawing board.

Will IT Build the New Front End for the Customer-Centric Enterprise?

To a far greater extent and much more quickly than anyone anticipated, companies are interacting with their customers through PCs, laptops, tablets, and mobile devices. Every company with customers has some kind of IT system, and increasingly those IT systems are being leveraged for customer-centric activities such as marketing, sales, and service.

The unexpectedly rapid transformation of IT from a mysterious back-office function to a high-profile enabler of multiple customer management services has been a shock to many CIOs. If you spent most of your career talking to the CFO, the idea of dealing with "the public" might seem unsettling.

The good news for CIOs, however, is that IT's elevation into an essential business function means that CIOs are more indispensable than ever before. Back in the old days, hiring a new CIO was mostly a headache for the CFO. Now, hiring a new CIO translates into guaranteed turmoil for the entire company and all of its business partners.

The new reliance on IT unquestionably elevates the role of the CIO. At the same time, it adds significantly to the CIO's responsibilities and ratchets up expectations that IT will perform as flawlessly as everyone's new smartphone.

In a very real sense, every CIO is competing with the ghost of Steve Jobs. Nowadays, people expect enterprise IT to work as well as consumer IT. But those expectations aren't always aligned with reality. Despite the chic elegance and futuristic design of your new tablet, it isn't nearly as complex or powerful as even the simplest enterprise IT systems.

As companies redirect more of their resources into providing unbeatable customer experiences, IT will become more deeply involved in customer-facing activities. At some companies, CIOs are already working closely with CMOs to make sure that each and every customer interaction is captured, measured, analyzed, optimized, and leveraged to benefit the company in a positive way. My hunch is that very soon, close working relationships between the CIO and the chief marketing officer (CMO) will be the norm and not the exception.

It also seems likely that IT will be called upon—sooner rather than later—to help the enterprise build an entirely new "front end" designed expressly for customer interactions. Those new customer interfaces won't be jury-rigged versions of traditional IT systems; they are more likely to be created from highly innovative combinations of hardware and software. Companies such as Google, Amazon, and Facebook have been hard at work building new and unorthodox IT systems, often by ripping apart hardware and rebuilding it to their own specifications.

It's only a matter of time before those innovations reach the market and become more widely available. When that happens, expectations will shoot through the roof. As the CIO, will you be ready to handle those higher expectations? Will you be ready to help the enterprise build the customer-facing IT systems of the future?

Smart Companies Leverage Innovation to Drive Value into the Business

I recently had a great conversation with Chris Miller, the CIO at Avanade. We were talking about the CIO's relationship with the C-suite, and Chris commented that while it's great to "have a seat at the table," the C-suite expects IT to deliver far more than just technology.

"Today, the expectation is that IT will drive innovation into the business, creating new revenue streams and new ways for engaging customers through technology," says Chris. "We've earned the seat at the table, but now we have to make contributions that are meaningful and significant."

Avanade is a leading a global business technology solutions and managed services provider. In his role as CIO, Chris is responsible for the leadership, management, and implementation of the technology capabilities that power the company's 21,000 professionals across more than 20 countries.

Chris serves as a trusted advisor both inside and outside the company. He and his team work closely with Microsoft to maintain Avanade's role as an aggressive early adopter of Microsoft enterprise technologies. The team regularly shares first-hand experience and insights about deployments with customers to help them optimize their own operations.

For example, Avanade recently helped Delta Air Lines improve its customer experience through an advanced mobile in-flight sales and service solution based on the Avanade Mobile Airline Platform. This end-to-end retail platform for airlines, jointly developed with Avanade's parent company, Accenture, combines Microsoft Dynamics for Retail software with Avanade's Connected Stores solution to help airlines improve how they serve customers while creating opportunities for new revenue.

Those kinds of innovation technology solutions are exactly what the C-suite looks for when it turns to the CIO for help. In both instances, the technology enabled a business outcome that drove new revenue.

"Executives are more savvy these days about technology, and they expect you to provide solutions that will help them grow the business," says Chris. "That's what having a seat at the table means today."

Great Firms Leverage the Skill and Expertise of Their CIOs Before Leaping into Newer Technologies

One of the great benefits of my role at HMG Strategy is that it gives me the opportunity to speak with many of the world's most respected IT leaders. Jeanette Horan and I spoke at length about the evolution of corporate IT and the role of the CIO in leading innovation across the enterprise.

Jeanette was recently appointed managing director of one of IBM's largest accounts. Previously, Jeanette served as IBM's chief information officer. As CIO, she was responsible for providing innovative capabilities for IBM's workforce, driving IT operational excellence for the enterprise, and supporting IBM's transformation agenda. Working in close partnership with senior management, she guided the development and implementation of a global technology strategy.

From my perspective, Jeanette is a truly transformational leader in every sense. One of the topics we discussed is how the CIO can provide exceptionally valuable advice and guidance to the business about newer technologies. Sometimes, we agreed, business leaders attempt to embrace technology that isn't quite ready for prime time. When that happens, problems can arise.

"IT has spent years integrating business processes and providing the seamless flow of information," says Jeanette. "You don't want to jeopardize all of that effort by setting up new information silos. That would be a giant step backward for the enterprise."

Some business leaders don't realize that when they contract independently with a SaaS provider, they risk "dis-integrating" the enterprise data management framework. The CIO, however, can help maintain the proper balance between the desire for innovation and the need for seamless integration.

"I'm a great proponent of software-as-a-service. It's great because you get to share the development costs and you don't have to worry about maintaining currency with operating systems and middleware, because that's all done by the vendor. But you have to see the big picture and understand how everything fits together," says Jeanette.

The hype around big data can be especially confusing to business leaders who seek quick gains in competitive markets. "There's a fallacy that big data somehow automatically gives you insight," says Jeanette. "You can have piles of data, but you won't get the insight until you know the right questions to ask. Usually, you need a data scientist or a statistical analyst to help you figure out the questions that will generate the insight you're looking for."

Jeanette also notes that even though an open-source data platform such as Hadoop is technically free, that doesn't mean you can operate it without incurring costs. "Just because you don't have to pay for a license doesn't mean it's free," says Jeanette. "You still have to connect it to everything else in your environment, you have to pay for the data, and you have to hire a data scientist to analyze the data. So it's not really free."

I genuinely appreciate Jeanette's candor and insight. Obviously, the cloud and big data have a lot to offer—and smart companies will continue leveraging the skills, experience, and expertise of their CIOs when making decisions about investing in new technology.

Getting Serious about Cybersecurity

There's no question that cybersecurity has become increasingly critical to the overall financial health of the modern enterprise. Every business, large and small, relies on a wide range of digital technologies, and all digital technologies can be compromised.

The 2014 Verizon Data Breach Investigations Report[3] offers a realistic overview of the multiple challenges we confront in our networked global economy. The report analyzed data from more than over 63,000 security incidents, including 1,367 confirmed data breaches. "The costs of a data breach can be enormous. And it's not just the remediation costs and potential fines; the damage to your reputation and loss of customer confidence could impact your success for years. Many companies never recover from a major data breach," the report states.

I urge you to download the report and share it with your team. It might also be a good idea to share the report with the C-suite and your board of directors. Cybersecurity risks can't be wished away. As a community of IT leaders, we need to face them head on and without illusions.

Another key problem is transparency. Since cyber crime is still considered embarrassing, it doesn't always get the attention it deserves and requires.

I use the word *embarrassing* because cyber crime often goes undetected for months and sometimes even years. Here's a great example: *The New York Times* recently reported on a cyber attack on JPMorgan Chase that potentially exposed confidential information regarding millions of individuals and small business. It "took the bank's security team more than two months to detect before it was stopped."[4]

According to the *Times,* luck played a large role in the discovery of the breach. "The intrusion at the nation's largest bank could have gone on for longer if not for a critical discovery by a Milwaukee security consulting firm." Apparently, a "loose-knit gang of Russian hackers" had gleaned passwords and e-mails from people who had registered to participate in the bank's Corporate Challenge races, which are held in major cities and are "open to bank employees and employees of other corporations." The security firm found a criminal database with billions of stolen passwords and usernames, apparently purloined by the hackers.

I urge you to read the *Times* story, which will leave you shaking your head in incredulity and wonderment. The bad guys are smart, imaginative, and thoroughly unscrupulous. Don't underestimate their abilities or their greed.

Hunting on the Network: Q&A with Cybersecurity Expert Shawn Henry of CrowdStrike

There's no question that cybersecurity has emerged as a major concern for modern companies. I sat down recently with my good friend Shawn Henry for a Q&A session about the role and responsibility of the CIO in dealing with the risks and dangers of cyber crime. A 24-year veteran of the FBI, Shawn is now president of the Services Division and chief security officer at CrowdStrike. Here is a condensed and lightly edited transcript of our excellent conversation:

Q: Shawn, would you explain the difference between offensive and proactive approaches to cybersecurity?

A: Offensive means you're leaving your network and you're chasing somebody who you believe has hacked your systems. It could also mean that you're actively outside your network trying to identify people who might be attacking your network. Proactive means that you're working in your environment, within your own network, and within your own perimeter to actively seek out and hunt for indicators that the adversaries are there, and that you're taking actions to mitigate threats on your own network.

Q: Why is it important for CIOs to understand the difference between offensive and proactive approaches?

A: Imagine the physical world. If a thief breaks into your building, it makes sense to look for clues inside the building and to find him before he does damage and gets away. That would be the proactive approach. The offensive approach, on the other hand, would be chasing the thief down the street and into another building. You don't have the authority to do that. It's a job for the police.

Q: How does all of this relate to the idea of "hunting on your network"?

A: For years, security protocols have been based on the concept of *defense in depth,* which means that you've got multiple layers of defense: a firewall, an intrusion detection system, an intrusion prevention system and multifactor authentication to get onto the network. You're layering your defenses to make it more difficult for the adversaries. We still need to continue doing that, but the simple truth is that sophisticated adversaries can get onto the best-protected networks.

The concept of hunting on your network means actually falling back from the perimeter and actively seeking out the adversaries within your environment, looking for indicators that you're under attack. The adversaries are stealthy. They're sophisticated. The tools they use and the tactics they use are highly complex. They are often difficult, if not impossible, to find.

You've got to use intelligence to understand who the adversaries are and what types of tools and techniques they're using. Then you can use technology and analytic techniques to look for indicators that they are in your network. If you can identify the adversaries, you can greatly mitigate the threat.

What we see in most of the cases where there have been significant breaches—in retail, financial services, manufacturing, and the defense industrial base—is that the adversaries have been on those networks for many months before data are exfiltrated. The reason is that it often takes months for adversaries to fully establish themselves within a network, identify the most valuable information on the network, and then exfiltrate the information off the network. Those processes can take months. Hunting on the network allows you to identify adversaries and take action swiftly before they exfiltrate your information. That's that concept.

Q: How can CIOs use data analytics to spot the indicators left by the bad guys?

A: You've got to look at a lot of data. You're looking at logs, at internal movement within the network, at processes running on the end point, anomalous behavior or activity that's occurring on desktops and laptops.

There are hundreds of millions of processes on a big network that are going to run every single day. Reviewing all of it is obviously beyond the capabilities of a human, but having analysts that know how to use the right tools will provide them visibility into the network and will identify red flags and anomalous behaviors that could be indicators of cyber crime.

As an example, let's say there's an employee who normally works 9–5 Monday through Friday, and all of a sudden you see this person logging in on Saturday morning at 2:00 A.M. That's unusual activity, but in and of itself, doesn't necessarily mean it's anything malicious. It could be the end of the quarter. Or maybe the employee is finishing up a big project or getting ready to go on vacation. But it's still a red flag that says, "Let's take a closer look at this."

When you look at it a little deeper, maybe you discover the employee's computer had an unusual executable that was downloaded the day before he started logging in at unusual hours. Then you look a little deeper, and you find out the employee's computer is making callouts to a domain that your network has never called before.

You start lining up those observations and looking at the aggregate data that you've collected. Sure enough, you discover that the employee's computer has been compromised—the adversaries have taken over the employee's account and are using it to steal information. Unfortunately, it's become a fairly common practice. One of the best ways to fight it is by looking at lots of data and searching for indicators of attack.

Q: Is good cyber defense similar to good fraud risk management control?

A: Yes, there are more similarities than differences. In the physical world, it takes lots of reconnaissance to mount large-scale frauds and heists. The bad guys spent lots of time collecting intelligence and information about the target. They spend lots of time planning their activities. It's very similar in the cyber world. Your adversaries put a lot of time and thought into figuring out ways to penetrate your cyber defenses. But they leave red flags. They leave signs and signals indicating their activities.

Q: And the CIO needs to know what those signs and signals are?

A: Yes. In the physical world, alarms go off when people try to break into your property. There are alarms in the cyber world, too. But you have to pay attention; you can't ignore them. You have to investigate and find out what's going on. Good cybersecurity is very similar to fraud risk management in the physical world.

Q: It sounds like there are ways to spot the bad guys.

A: Yes, there are red flags and indicators. That's what hunting on the network is about—paying attention to what's happening around you, inside the network. Organizations naturally tend to focus on the perimeter. But we can't be naïve and expect the perimeter to stop everything. We have to accept the fact that adversaries will get inside the perimeter. We need to develop proactive processes and policies for dealing with threats inside the network.

Q: The media focus on cases in which credit card information is stolen, but the theft of intellectual property (IP) is potentially much more dangerous. Do companies need to focus more on protecting IP?

A: Absolutely, you're exactly right. Credit card theft is relatively easy to quantify. And you know fairly quickly when it happens. When IP is stolen, it can take years before you realize it or begin seeing the impact. Unlike credit card theft, IP theft is harder to quantify. As a result, it gets less attention.

But companies are valued because of their IP. Think about the major technology companies—their valuation is largely based on the strength of their intellectual property. Their IP is their competitive advantage in the market; it's what they sell to make money. If their IP is stolen—and if somebody else is able to manufacture their products for pennies on the dollar—that represents an enormous and potentially catastrophic loss. The impact of IP theft is huge. There is also a national security aspect. If an adversary steals IP about a critical defense system, the entire nation could be exposed to risk.

Q: In your presentations, you talk about the important of detecting, identifying, and mitigating cyber threats. Could you touch briefly on each of those aspects?

A: The detection piece is really about looking for those indicators of attack. What's the unusual behavior? What types of malware are being deployed? Are we seeing communications outside the network to domains that we would typically never visit, which indicates an adversary is using those computers for command and control? Where do we see these unusual logins by people who have no reason to be logging in? Those are the indicators of attack, and that's where you come up with detection.

The investigation piece is when you see those indicators and the red flag goes off, give it a second look. Don't ignore the alarm. Take a look, pay attention, and make sure that you're getting eyes on glass.

Mitigation is all about rendering the environment safe, making sure the adversary has been removed from the network, replacing malware with clean software, and then monitoring the network to make sure the adversary doesn't come back in.

Q: Generally speaking, what's the best way for a CIO to build an effective response process, and what should that process include?

A: First of all, it starts with having a plan and understanding that it's likely you're going to have a breach. So you need to have a breach plan that covers remediating the network, communicating with external partners, and making the network environment safe again.

You need to make sure you have appropriate controls in place, appropriate practices that not only defend the network but also detect anomalies within the network.

You need the right technology because technology is what gives you visibility into the network environment.

You also need people who are properly trained, who understand the risks, and who know how the adversaries operate. You also need to know your own network. Many companies have acquired other networks through mergers or acquisitions. Sometimes, those companies have no idea where their gateways are. They have no idea where their domain controllers are. They have no idea how many endpoints they have on the network. You can't defend your property if you don't know where it is. That's a fundamental aspect of protecting the network. You can't defend what you don't know.

Q: There's the idea that the government should somehow be involved in all of this and that the government is going to protect us from cyber crime. What's the argument in favor of corporations protecting themselves and taking responsibility themselves for doing a better job of fighting cyber crime?

A: This is something that's very important to me. Let's talk about the physical world again. The government's fundamental responsibility is protecting citizens. We have police forces that patrol. We have fire departments and emergency medical technicians that respond to emergencies. Government protects the citizens and provides essential services.

We also expect people to take care of their responsibilities. We lock our houses at night. We turn on our alarm systems. We make sure the neighbor picks up our mail when we go on vacation. We take general precautions.

Similarly, in the cyber world, organizations need to protect themselves. But government has neither the authority nor the resources to block adversaries from our networks. The private sector has to protect itself.

The government can do more. It can change certain policies. It can engage more with other governments to curtail corporate espionage and encourage fair business practices. We can hold government accountable for fulfilling its proper role. But the private sector needs to protect itself from adversaries in the cyber world. That's the reality today.

Dealing with Cyber Crime Requires a Realistic Mindset

At the beginning of this chapter, I wrote briefly about my conversations with Israel Martinez, a leading voice in the global cybersecurity industry. We had an in-depth follow-up discussion shortly before the book manuscript was finalized, and I want to share his additional thoughts concerning the challenges of cybersecurity in a digitally connected world.

Our follow-up conversation covered a wide range of topics within the realm of cybersecurity. We began by discussing the viability of *defense in depth* approaches to cybersecurity. Here are some highlights of the many valuable insights he shared in our conversation:

"Defense in depth is about layering security across the organization. That concept still works. What's happened is

the layers are more complicated. As an example, we used to work with a model that had a few simple layers: data, application, host, and network. But now the model has grown to include a perimeter layer, an internal layer, a vulnerability layer, a user layer, and a business layer."

Israel says that the cloud adds complexity to the model. "In the past, people would look at cybersecurity as either black or white. Now we see lots of gray areas. It's more integrated and complicated today."

"Defense in depth is still a good model, but the tools we're using to defend against bad guys have changed dramatically. One of the tools that most companies are still not using effectively is what we call intelligence. What is intelligence? Intelligence is really information that the bad guy has about your information and your network that you don't know about. It's pretty simple. If you're going into battle, you want to know what the other guy knows about you."

Israel says, "For example, many security compromises go unnoticed for two years before they're discovered. That's a long time, and it gives the enemy a big head start. Visualize this; the bad actor is in the network, exfiltrating data, and the victim doesn't know about it until something tangible (bad) happens."

The bad guys aren't standing still. Israel says that they are constantly innovating and trying to stay ahead of the good guys. "When we identify a new kind of malware, we give it a name and we train our systems to recognize it. Then we call it signatured malware. *But as soon as we do that, the bad guys modify the malware and it then becomes* unsignatured malware. *That means we have to go through the process of detection all over again. It's a cycle, and we need to learn how to respond more rapidly and more effectively than we did in the past."*

That's why intelligence is important. Israel says, *"We need to know today what the bad guys know. We can't wait for two years to find out what the bad guys are doing inside of our network and what they are learning about us."*

Israel explained to me that much of the actionable intelligence necessary to mount a practical defense against cyber criminals can be gathered using "open source" methods and resources. *"The Internet is like an iceberg. The average person only experiences the top 10 percent of it. Underneath, there's a* darknet *that is largely unseen by normal users. That's where a lot of the bad guys love to hide. The good news is that we— the good guys—have learned to navigate that dark area of the Internet. We can watch the bad guys and see how they're exchanging information."*

"We've partnered with domestic and international organizations that know how to legally watch threat activity and malware in subtle ways, which means that the bad guys don't know they're being watched. That enables the good guys to identify unsignatured malware long before an attack is launched."

Israel says, *"The ability to identify incoming threats and take proactive measures has a potentially large financial impact, since it enables organizations to spend less money on costly perimeter defenses. Ideally, spending should be reallocated to fund more targeted types of proactive-defensive strategies."*

He identified a need to shift from a defense model to a proactive defense. *Israel defined it this way: "A proactive defense is not an 'offense,' which implies some kind of malicious damage and is against the law. Proactive defense is real-time reaction to threat actors via integrating threat intelligence into a cyber resiliency plan. This requires innovative strategies like integrating actionable intelligence into an automated threat response system."*

CIOs need actionable intelligence—that is, "real-time information about where the bad guy is currently attacking or already infiltrated via advanced methods often undetectable by current internal analysis tools. This knowledge truncates the average two years to discover a breach. That puts you in a more powerful position because you're then spending more money in the right areas—where the bad guys are actually punching holes and compromising your systems."

Despite the availability of newer strategies to counter cyber crime, many companies still rely on traditional methods. In some ways, it's not surprising to discover that inertia often slows efforts to fight cyber crime. I found Israel's insight in this area especially interesting: "The corporate culture has to change. At large companies, CIOs and CISOs are still too concerned about the liability of acknowledging compromises and are incented to get things done on a project-by-project albeit strategic basis to show "due care" in cyber defense. Goals, objectives, plans, and activities are often planned around a quarterly schedule. So we're incenting key players not to shift gears (directions) quickly, but to keep a steady pace and focus on long-term compliance."

Israel says, "Here's the problem with the traditional approach: The bad guys aren't working on a quarterly timetable. The bad guys aren't working on any timetable or schedule. They are working nonstop to innovate and compromise our systems at will, and that makes us vulnerable. Another problem we face is that our private sector and our government sectors are not closely aligned to manage the cybersecurity challenge. In some countries, the government—including the military—works closely with private industry to exploit weaknesses in our cyber defenses."

As a result, we see evidence of what some experts describe as the largest transfer of wealth in history. Israel says, "It's not just privacy information, cash, and financial information that's being stolen. Intellectual property is exfiltrated. The cost of losing intellectual property has long-term effects. It can cripple a company. It makes it harder to compete over time."

I asked Israel to list three major hurdles that prevent companies from dealing effectively with cyber crime. Here's what he told me:

1. Most boards don't know that their companies are already experiencing economic cyber warfare and their networks have already been breached.

2. Although many people think that technology will solve the problem, it won't.

3. Many put faith in the government to solve the problem, but it can't. It doesn't have the mandate or the resources.

Here's what Israel said about these misconceptions:

Those three misconceptions must change for effective risk mitigation. The new axioms should be: One, cyber threats will not just go away it will get worse before it gets better, so stop looking for blame and learn methods to more quickly integrate innovation. Two, compliance is not enough; over 50 percent of today's cybersecurity spending is in the wrong areas, so let's change that. Three, let's be honest about the state of cybersecurity. Be a team player and report advanced malware and targeted attacks across industries and yes, even with the government. Do it early and often so we can expedite the response cycle. The reality is that government sees the private sector as the "front-line," and we all need complete information regarding threat intelligence so we can be more effective.

When I listen to board requests, I hear them ask about cyber risk strategies and principles, not about operational technology. So it's about perspective. Trying to fix the cyber crime problem solely with technology is like a plumber trying to strategically manage water for the city by finding every leaky faucet in New York. It's not going to happen. So you must change perspective and use enterprise risk management tools and executive perspective and strategies to succeed.

Part of the solution is education. We need to do a better job of educating boards about the realities of the digital economy. Cybersecurity vulnerabilities are actually symptoms of the velocity of technology innovation, which is a new order of the digital revolution. Executives and board members need to understand how the pace of the innovation has accelerated and will continue to impact their business. The traditional methodologies and governance models are antiquated. If we really want to succeed, we need to learn how to innovate faster than the bad guys and be willing to see beyond the horizon how cyber innovation is going to impact the marketplace and us individually.

Smart companies, says Israel, will adopt a "cyber warfare mindset," and begin looking at the world from a more realistic perspective. It's important to know that not all cyber criminals are equal in terms of skills, resources, or intentions. Cyber criminals from Eastern Bloc nations, for instance, tend to hunt for cash and credit card information. Cyber criminals from Asia, on the other hand, might look for industrial secrets and other forms of intellectual property. Most frightening are cyber criminals from the Middle East or *hactivists,* who seem to be looking for ways to hack into power grids and public utilities to cause critical infrastructure damage.

The world has changed immeasurably since the development of the modern digital computer. The Internet and the Web have brought us closer together and changed the way we live. The cloud, social, and mobile have added to the richness and complexity of our lives.

At the same time that technology has opened new doors of opportunity for billions of people, its social impact is accelerating. Cyber crime poses real threats, both in social and economic terms. As a community, we need to become more aware of the risks and dangers, and we need to address them directly.

Focusing on Future Trends

I asked my friend Greg Fell to talk briefly about two areas that probably deserve more attention from CIOs. Greg is the former CIO of Terex Corp. These days, he works as a venture capitalist and investor in tech startups, so he's keenly aware of what's new and exciting in the field. Here are some highlights of Greg's comments:

> *The Internet of Things (IoT) is a hot topic right now for everybody. The IoT is really a platform for big data generated by billions of sensors in devices and machines. You're talking about collecting and analyzing massive amounts of information, and then translating it into business value. CIOs need to be looking more closely at the IoT and figuring out how they can use it to generate value.*
>
> *If your company has customers, then you've got a use case for the IoT. Every one of your customers generates information, and you can use that information to make better decisions about serving your customers and selling to your customers. The IoT is a perfect place for gathering customer information, which makes the IoT critical to any outward-facing business strategy. It's up to the CIO to figure out how to use the IoT to create more business value for the company.*
>
> *The idea of putting sensors on devices and machines isn't new. What's new is that the cost of sensors has fallen dramatically, thanks to Moore's law. Analyzing sensor data creates all kinds of possibilities, including the idea of predictive maintenance. GE is pushing the envelope in that area, developing systems that predict when parts will fail so there's*

never any unplanned downtime. If you're operating a gas turbine, a wind generator, or a jet aircraft engine, you want zero unplanned downtime. The IoT takes the idea of zero unplanned downtime and turns it into something possible and practical. Those are the kinds of opportunities that CIOs need to be looking for.

When I was in the automotive industry, we had sensors on some machines, but they were very expensive and the networks required to collect information from them were also expensive. All of that is much easier and much cheaper today. It's amazing how much information you can get from a relatively inexpensive sensor. In many cases, customers will give you information for free in exchange for a smartphone app. As the CIO, you really need to be looking at how the IoT can benefit your business. From my perspective, the IoT is part of the big shift from inward-facing to outward-facing IT strategy. It fundamentally transforms how you use data.

Greg also made the point that CIOs need to shift their attention away from traditional IT systems that looked at the past and begin thinking more about systems designed to analyze real-time data and generate insights that can be used by the business. "It's happening in every field. It's about using sensors and scanners to generate real-time business information. It's about knowing when a consumer takes a box of cereal off a shelf and then restocking the shelf automatically. This isn't some kind of futuristic vision—this is the new competitive landscape. The companies that figure out how to use data most effectively will be the winners in this new economy."

3D printing is also on Greg's radar. 3D printing is a sex-ier version of the term *additive manufacturing*, which began in the 1980s and has steadily gained momentum. Today, it's fair to say that 3D printing is on the edge of "breaking out" and becoming a practical process for the production of many items. Since 3D printing processes are guided by software, it's only a matter of time before IT becomes involved.

When most people think about 3D printing, they imagine making small things out of plastic. "But the reality is that 3D printing will become a significant driver of economic growth in the very near future. Today, we're printing cell phone covers from plastic. Tomorrow, we'll be printing replacement parts from metal. That will be a sea change."

Greg says, "Just think of the savings in shipping costs. Soon, you won't have to order replacement parts and wait for them to arrive—you'll be able to print them out whenever you need them. That will become a reality sooner than many people expect. The need for warehousing spare parts will diminish. With 3D printing, manufacturers will create new parts on demand and ship them as needed."

"Not everyone will have a 3D printer at home or at the office. For some businesses, it will make more sense to order an item from a manufacturer's website and pick it up at an intermediary location equipped with a 3D printer." Greg thinks that companies "like Staples or Office Max might decide to offer that kind of service. This will be an emerging business model, and it will likely become a new channel for businesses to connect with their customers. CIOs need

to begin thinking about those kinds of business models and figuring out how they might impact their companies.

"It's all part of the big shift, and CIOs need to pay attention. In a very real sense, we're seeing parts of the e-commerce economy moving back into the physical world. In addition to downloading information, we'll be downloading products. CIOs can play a major role in this transformation because it can't happen without the active participation of IT."

Greg says, "It will also require new ways of thinking about monetizing IP. What's more valuable, the original design for a product or the code you make available to consumers so they can manufacture it on their 3D printers? That's a fascinating question. CIOs will need to begin re-prioritizing information based on the answer. CIOs will need to start thinking ahead of the curve and make certain that IP is properly locked down. Today, cyber criminals can only steal your information. What happens when they can also steal your products?"

CIOs, says Greg, need to spend more time imagining the future and envisioning the impact of emerging trends on their companies. Staying ahead of the curve requires thinking about changes that will unfold over the short term, the middle term and the long term. I like how Greg wraps up the challenges ahead of us: "In five years, we might have replicators in our homes and so maybe you should begin thinking about how that will impact your business. Within 12 months, you'll probably be able to order 3D printed parts or small items and pick them up at Staples, so you should definitely be thinking now about how that will affect or disrupt your business."

Greg says, "Fairly soon, it will become common for people to have medical sensors in their bodies. Physicians will inject nanobots into cancer patients to destroy malignant cells and repair damaged tissue. Advances in medicine will spread to other industries, creating new efficiencies, new opportunities, and new disruptions. Our world is changing rapidly; we need to begin thinking now about how we want to incorporate new technologies into our IT systems. It's a responsibility that we can't ignore."

Five Key Trends that Are Fundamentally Transforming IT Leadership

IT is changing: Are you ready for the challenges ahead? Sheila Jordan is CIO at Symantec, a global leader in security, backup, and availability solutions. A Fortune 500 company, Symantec employs 20,000 workers in 50 countries and operates one of the largest global data-intelligence networks.

I spoke recently with Sheila, and she told me that she sees five key trends influencing the IT industry and accelerating transformation.

"Today, since everyone has a mobile phone which serves as mini-desktop in their pocket, mobility is the first major trend. The second key trend is cloud computing—cloud is everywhere. The third big trend is data. We've been using structured data for years, but unstructured data has become increasingly relevant to decision-making in the modern enterprise," says Sheila.

"The fourth trend is the Internet of Things. By 2020, there will be 26 billion connected devices. In addition to sensors in devices, there will be wearable devices. The Internet of Things will create radical changes for IT in the enterprise," says Sheila. "The fifth and most interesting trend—and possibly the most challenging—is around identities. Our personal and professional identities are converging. The whole notion of identities is evolving. This will pose huge challenges—and great opportunities—for CIOs, all over the world."

Although most CIOs are aware of those five trends, they tend to think about them independently. The tendency by CIOs to regard the five trends as separate phenomena will make it more difficult to identify and provide the most effective solutions.

"CIOs need to focus on the data that's moving between all of those systems and applications," says Sheila. "And of course, the data needs to be secure. From my perspective, CIOs should focus on securing and protecting data as it moves—not just around the enterprise, but beyond the four walls of the enterprise."

CIOs also need to focus on making sure that data is relevant to business users. "Data has to add value and drive good decisions," says Sheila. "Data has become a strategic asset, and we need to make sure that it's available when and where people need it."

I also asked Sheila to describe the most significant leadership challenges facing CIOs in the modern enterprise.

"Leadership in my opinion is really all about follow-ship," says Sheila. "A leader has to paint the vision and communicate the strategy so that it makes sense and is realistic, reasonable, and attainable. And you have to keep messaging your strategy to all levels of the organization, and to all of your constituencies. You need to be really clear about your strategy, and then communicate it—over and over—to all the different audiences you serve. You have to just keep communicating that strategy."

I genuinely appreciate Sheila's common sense approach to the business of CIO leadership, and her emphasis on communicating clearly and effectively across the multiple constituencies of the twenty-first-century enterprise. Sheila's advice is not only useful, it's essential for dealing successfully with the momentous trends that are fundamentally transforming our industry.

Notes

1. McKinsey & Company and World Economic Forum, Risk and Responsibility in a Hyperconnected World, World Economic Forum (January 2014), p. 3, http://

reports.weforum.org/hyperconnected-world-2014
/wp-content/blogs.dir/37/mp/files/pages/files/final-15
-01-risk-and-responsibility-in-a-hyperconnected-world
-report.pdf.

2. Ibid., p. 3.

3. http://www.verizonenterprise.com/DBIR/2014/

4. Matthew Goldstein and Nicole Perlroth, "Luck Played
Role in Discovery of Data Breach at JPMorgan Affecting
Millions," The New York Times (October 31, 2014),
http://dealbook.nytimes.com/2014/10/31/discovery-of
-jpmorgan-cyberattack-aided-by-company-that-runs-race
-website-for-bank/?emc=eta1&_r=0.

RECOMMENDED READING

Adams, James L. *Conceptual Blockbusting: A Guide to Better Ideas.* 4th ed. New York: Basic Books, 2001.

Barlow, Mike, and David B. Thomas. *The Executive's Guide to Enterprise Social Media Strategy: How Social Networks Are Radically Transforming Your Business.* Hoboken, NJ: John Wiley & Sons, 2011.

Berkun, Scott. *The Myths of Innovation.* Sebastopol, CA: O'Reilly Media, 2010.

Carr, Nicholas. *Does IT Matter?: Information Technology and the Corrosion of Competitive Advantage.* Boston, Harvard Business review Press, 2004.

—"IT Doesn't Matter." Boston: Harvard Business Review, May 2003.

—*The Big Switch: Rewiring the World, from Edison to Google.* New York: W. W. Norton, 2008.

Christensen, Clayton M. *The Innovator's Dilemma: The Revolutionary Book That Will Change the Way You Do Business.* New York: HarperBusiness, 2000.

Christensen, Clayton M., and Michael E. Raynor. *The Innovator's Solution: Creating and Sustaining Successful Growth.* Boston: Harvard Business Review Press, 2003.

Cohen, Jared, and Eric Schmidt. *The New Digital Age: Transforming Nations, Businesses and Our Lives.* New York: First Vintage Books, 2014.

Collins, Jim. *Good to Great: Why Some Companies Make the Leap ... and Others Don't.* New York: HarperCollins, 2001.

Cukler, Kenneth, and Viktor Mayer-Schönberger. *Big Data: A Revolution That Will Transform How We Live, Work, and Think.* Boston: Mariner Books, 2014.

Diamandis, Peter H., and Steven Kotler. *Abundance: The Future Is Better Than You Think.* New York: Free Press, 2012.

Drucker, Peter. Innovation and Entrepreneurship. New York: Harper & Row, 1985.

Duhigg, Charles. *The Power of Habit: Why We Do What We Do in Life and Business*. New York: Random House, 2012.

Dyer, Jeff, Hal Gregersen, and Clayton M. Christensen. *The Innovator's DNA: Mastering the Five Skills of Disruptive Innovators*. Boston: Harvard Business Review Press, 2011.

GE, *GE Global Innovation Barometer 2014—Insight on Disruption Collaboration and the Future of Work*, http://www.ideaslaboratory.com/projects/innovation-barometer-2014/

Gertner, Jon. *The Idea Factory: Bell Labs and the Great Age of American Innovation*. New York: Penguin Books, 2012.

Gladwell, Malcolm. *Outliers: The Story of Success*. New York: Little, Brown, 2008.

Gross, Daniel. *Better, Stronger, Faster: The Myth of American Decline and the Rise of a New Economy*. New York: Free Press, 2012.

Hamel, Gary. *What Matters Now: How to Win in a World of Relentless Change, Ferocious Competition, and Unstoppable Innovation*. San Francisco: Jossey-Bass, 2012.

Heath, Chip, and Dan Heath. *Made to Stick: Why Some Ideas Survive and Others Die*. New York: Random House, 2007.

Isaacson, Walter. *Steve Jobs*. New York: Simon & Schuster, 2011.

Johnson, Steven. *Where Good Ideas Come From: The Natural History of Innovation*. New York: Riverhead Books, 2010.

Kahneman, Daniel. *Thinking, Fast and Slow*. New York: Farrar, Straus and Giroux, 2011.

Kelley, Tom, with Jonathan Littman. *The Art of Innovation: Lessons in Creativity from IDEO, America's Leading Design Firm*. New York: Doubleday, 2001.

Kotter, John P. *Leading Change*. Boston: Harvard Business School Press, 1996.

Minelli, Michael, Michele Chambers, and Ambiga Dhiraj. *Big Data, Big Analytics: Emerging Business Intelligence and Analytic Trends for Today's Businesses*. Hoboken, NJ: John Wiley & Sons, 2013.

Moore, Geoffrey A. *Dealing with Darwin: How Great Companies Innovate at Every Phase of Their Evolution*. New York: Portfolio/Penguin, 2005, 2008.

Prahalad, C. K., and M. S. Krishnan. *The New Age of Innovation: Driving Co-created Value Through Global Networks*. New York: McGraw-Hill, 2008.

Ridley, Matt. *The Rational Optimist: How Prosperity Evolves*. New York: HarperCollins, 2010.

Rosenstein, Bruce. *Living in More Than One World: How Peter Drucker's Wisdom Can Inspire and Transform Your Life*. San Francisco: Berrett-Koehler, 2009.

Senor, Dan, and Saul Singer. *Start-up Nation: The Story of Israel's Economic Miracle*. New York: Twelve/Hachette Book Group, 2011.

Tapscott, Don, and Anthony D. Williams. *Macrowikinomics: New Solutions for a Connected Planet*. New York: Portfolio/Penguin, 2010.

—Wikinomics: *How Mass Collaboration Changes Everything*. New York: Portfolio/Penguin, 2008.

MEET OUR EXPERT SOURCES

Rich Adduci is senior vice president and chief information officer (CIO) at Boston Scientific. In his role as CIO, Rich has led the transformation of Boston Scientific's IS organization, creating a global IS organization focused on delivering competitive advantage for Boston Scientific through the innovative use of information and technology. This transformational journey was featured in the book *The Transformation CIO: Leadership and Innovation Strategies for IT Executives in a Rapidly Changing World* by Hunter Muller. Adduci is actively engaged in shaping direction in the information technology community at large through his role on several advisory groups, including the SAP Life Sciences Advisory Committee, and serves as a member of the board of directors for the GHX Healthcare Exchange. In 2012 and 2013, he was named as one of *CIO Magazine*'s top 100 CIOs and also ranked #5 in the top 100 CIOs by ExecuRank. He is a champion of inclusion and diversity in the workplace and was named as the 2013 Diversity Executive Sponsor of the year by Boston Scientific. Adduci actively supports his community; among his community outreach is his membership on the Boston American Heart Association board of directors since 2007. He was selected as the Boston American Heart Association board chair in 2012.

Prior to joining Boston Scientific, Adduci was a partner at Accenture, where he had an 18-year career. He holds more than 15 European patents and two US patents for the development of modeling tools to support business strategy and market entry for new wireless technologies.

Adduci earned a BS in industrial engineering from Purdue University in 1988 and an MBA from the University of Chicago in 1993 with concentrations in finance and economics. He was recently honored as a Purdue Outstanding Industrial Engineer, a distinction limited to less than 1 percent of all industrial engineering graduates at Purdue.

* * *

F. Thaddeus Arroyo is CEO of AT&T Mexico, LLC., and the former chief information officer (CIO) at AT&T. In that role, Arroyo oversaw systems supporting all AT&T business segments and global compute and storage services. In addition to directing the company's internal information technology organization and internal and external customer-hosting data centers, he was responsible for AT&T's digital properties and capabilities across all business segments.

Arroyo has successfully advanced AT&T's IT transformation strategy from integration, rationalization, and capabilities development to an innovation-fueled organization focused on transforming business processes and market offerings in ways that create new value and velocity for AT&T's business, customers, and partners. Under Arroyo's leadership, AT&T has been consistently recognized for thought leadership and creativity in information technology innovation and execution. Awards include the Information Week 500 for six consecutive years and the CIO 100 Award in six of the last seven years. AT&T was also recognized by *Computerworld* as one of the 100 best companies to work for in IT for 2012 and 2013.

Arroyo has been recognized by numerous publications for his contributions to the IT industry through thought leadership, innovation, and creativity in planning and deploying technology.

* * *

Ramón Baez is senior vice president and chief information officer (CIO) of HP, responsible for the global information technology (IT) strategy and all of the company's IT assets that support HP employees and help drive strategic company priorities. This includes worldwide application development, the company's private cloud, IT security, data management, technology infrastructure, and telecommunication networks.

His career spans more than three decades with global Fortune 100 companies in industries including manufacturing, packaged goods, aerospace and defense, and products and services for the scientific community. Prior to HP, he was vice president of information technology services and CIO of Kimberly-Clark Corp., where he was responsible for leading the company's enterprise-wide information systems initiatives. Before Kimberly-Clark, Baez served in CIO roles for Thermo Fisher Scientific, Inc. and Honeywell's Automation and Control Solution group. He began his career at Northrop

Grumman, where he spent 25 years and finished as CIO for its electronics systems sensor sector.

Baez graduated from the University of La Verne in California with a bachelor's degree in business administration.

*   *   *

Dr. Ashwin Ballal has been vice president and chief information officer at KLA-Tencor since 2009. Prior to which, Dr. Ballal was president and managing director for KLA-Tencor India from 2007. He began at KLA-Tencor in 2000 and has held various executive and senior level positions, including those in marketing, engineering, program and operations management. During his tenure with the company, he was also General Manager for the Macro Inspection Product Division with full P&L responsibilities. Before joining KLA-Tencor, he held various senior management positions at Electroglas Inc., Keithley Instruments, and Noran Instruments.

He earned his doctorate and post-doctorate degrees in material science and engineering from the University of Maryland at College Park and his bachelor's degree in metallurgy from the National Institute of Technology in India. Dr. Ballal lives in San Jose, California, with his wife, Sandhya, daughter, Shyna, and son, Shawnuk. He is an avid sports enthusiast and loves to travel to exotic locations around the world with his family.

*   *   *

Linda Ban is the Global C-Suite Study director for the IBM Institute for Business Value (IBV). Her background includes more than 25 years in information technology, business and operations strategy, and systems development. Her career focus has been in anticipating the next "new thing" and bridging the technical and business sides of the organization—ensuring that technology solutions support the objectives of the enterprise as a whole. Ban has extensive experience in running large programs, ranging from enterprise system implementations and upgrades to organization-wide communication networks. In addition to these roles, she also has extensive experience in creating, implementing, and overseeing the accompanying organizations that provide operational support for both the technical and business side of these functions.

In her current role as the Global C-Suite Study director, Ban provides the leadership, strategy, and program oversight for the overall IBM C-Suite Study program within IBV, where IBM has interviewed more than 23,000 C-suite executives face-to-face during the last nine years. She works with global teams to focus on trend identification and strategies that address critical business challenges faced by companies globally. In addition to her leadership role for the overall program, she has published extensively on a broad range of business topics, challenges, and solutions.

* * *

Mike Benson is the executive vice president and chief information officer for DIRECTV, Inc. He is responsible for creating and maintaining information technology solutions for DIRECTV's business operations nationwide. He oversees reporting, analysis and infrastructure requirements, customer billing and payment systems, as well as customer care systems and financial, marketing, sales, and decision support.

Before joining DIRECTV, Benson held a variety of executive-level positions at AT&T Wireless, where he had cross-enterprise responsibility for the company's information technology and national real-estate organizations. Most recently, as executive vice president and CIO, he directed a worldwide reengineering of AT&T Wireless's internal service-based IT organization from 2000 to 2003. In 2000, as vice president of IT Infrastructure and Operations, Benson established technical direction for the company's IT infrastructure team to support business growth through major acquisitions by initiating service quality programs and crisis management frameworks.

He worked for McCaw Cellular Communications from 1987 until 1995, when the company was acquired by AT&T Wireless. As vice president of Information Services, he led the development of the region's information systems organization supporting significant business. During his service as director of development for McCaw's cellular division, Benson translated customer and organizational objectives into technology strategies and reduced billing expenses by 50 percent division-wide.

Prior to his career in wireless communications, Benson served as manager of development for Advance Technology

Laboratories in Redmond and Bothell, Washington. Earlier career experience included a position as a senior systems analyst in the frozen food packing and distribution industry with J.R. Simplot, Inc.

* * *

Vic Bhagat is executive vice president, Enterprise Business Solutions, and chief information officer at EMC Corporation. With revenues of $21.7 billion in 2012 and more than 60,000 people worldwide, EMC is a global leader in enabling businesses and service providers to transform their operations and deliver IT-as-a-service. Fundamental to this transformation is cloud computing. Through innovative products and services, EMC accelerates the journey to cloud computing, helping IT departments to store, manage, protect, and analyze their most valuable asset—information—in a more agile, trusted, and cost-efficient way.

A 30-year industry veteran, Bhagat joined EMC in January 2013 to lead EMC's Information Technology, Global Centers of Excellence, Global Business Services, and Indirect Procurement organizations. Together, he and the global, unified Enterprise Business Solutions team will be responsible for providing the technology, services, and support to enable EMC to optimize enterprise processes; furthering global sales and R&D relationships in BRIC and emerging countries; and delivering world-class services that drive innovation and revenue generation for EMC. This not only includes continuing to evolve EMC's own IT organization but advancing its award-winning IT Proven program to enable customers and partners to truly transform from silo-driven data centers into the IT organizations of the future.

Prior to joining EMC, he spent more than 20 years at GE, where he served as CIO for multiple GE organizations, including GE Aviation Services, GE Global Growth and Operations, CNBC, GE Corporate, and GE India and Southeast Asia. Along the way, he not only drove the company's IT strategies but managed large, global shared-services applications; built a technology center focused on high-end technology and digital solutions; and fueled GE's global innovation, opening numerous Centers of Excellence focused on big data, digital analytics, and digital strategies. Prior to joining EMC, Bhagat helped establish Accenture's worldwide big data analytics practice for natural resources.

Bhagat earned his bachelor's degree in information management and marketing from the University of Louisville and a diploma in physics and mathematics from Agra University in India. He previously served on several advisory boards, including AT&T Utilities & Field Services and Fairfield University—School of Software Engineering, and worked closely with University of Connecticut's School of Business.

* * *

Asheem Chandna is a partner at Greylock Partners, a leading venture capital firm, where he is focused on the next generation of enterprise IT companies. He has helped create and grow multiple technology businesses to market-leading positions—both as a venture capitalist and previously as a product executive. His current company boards include AppDynamics, Aquantia, Delphix, Imperva (IMPV), Palo Alto Networks (PANW), Zenprise, and Xsigo. He was previously on the boards of CipherTrust (INTC), NetBoost (INTC), PortAuthority (WBSN), Securent (CSCO), and Sourcefire (FIRE). Chandna joined Greylock from Check Point Software (CHKP), where he was vice-president of business development and product management.

*   *   *

Lee Feinberg founded DecisionViz in 2012 to help clients become great communicators of data and build leadership around the hardest aspects of data visualization—the necessary people, process, and culture changes. Based on his 20 years working in analytics and visualization, Lee developed the company's core services: The Blue Ocean for Visualization™ Framework and the DRAW-ON™ Method.

Feinberg runs the NJ and NY Tableau Software User Groups and served on Tableau's customer advocacy board. Industry leaders frequently ask Lee to address domestic and international audiences, including Tableau Software, O'Reilly Strata, TDWI, DMA, and TechTarget. Prior to founding DecisionViz, he led Nokia's Decision Planning and Visualization practice and was a strategy director and analytics lead at two top digital agencies, Digitas and Razorfish.

He received a BS and MS from Cornell University and has been awarded a US patent. Lee is a founding member and active advisor to Stevens Institute's Business Intelligence & Analytics program.

* * *

Greg Fell is an investor and highly regarded thought leader in the global IT community. He formally advises several technology startup companies, and mentors young entrepreneurs on the challenges in starting a technology business.

Previously, Fell served as vice president and chief information officer of Terex Corporation, where he led a strategic transformation of the IT organization. Terex is a manufacturer of industrial equipment that employs 23,000 persons in 50 manufacturing locations around the globe.

Fell is a graduate of Michigan State University, and spent several years on staff in the College of Engineering as a senior research programmer and instructor. He is the author of *Decoding the IT Value Problem: An Executive Guide for Achieving Optimal ROI on Critical IT Investments* (John Wiley & Sons, 2013).

* * *

Jay Ferro, chief information officer for the American Cancer Society, is responsible for the people, strategy, and operations of the global information technology of the organization. He is a recognized technology leader, known for creating and executing strategic visions to achieve business goals. He joined the Society executive staff in 2012, bringing a deep personal connection to the fight against cancer. In 2007, he founded the nonprofit group Priscilla's Promise, in honor of his late wife, who died from cancer. Priscilla's Promise raises funds for cervical cancer education and research; Jay currently serves as the group's executive director.

Prior to joining the Society, Ferro served as senior vice president and chief information officer for AdCare Health Systems, a rapidly growing and recognized innovator in healthcare facility management. He spent the previous seven years at AIG (American International Group), most recently as vice president and chief information officer for AIG Aviation, a leading global aerospace insurer. At AIG, he implemented numerous improvements that have delivered substantial value to the organization while managing significant organizational change in a turbulent market environment. In addition to his role as associate vice president of Information Technology with AIG Personal Lines, Ferro was selected as chief financial officer for operations and systems in 2006, and led multiple global IT finance and governance standards initiatives that resulted in millions of dollars in savings for the organization.

Known as a thought leader in the information technology arena, Ferro is a frequent guest speaker and panelist, both in Atlanta and nationwide. In recognition of his accomplishments, he was selected as Georgia CIO of the Year in 2011, and is currently serving as chair for the Georgia CIO Leadership Association. His commitment and dedication to community involvement is evidenced by the time and energy he contributes. In addition to his work with Priscilla's Promise, in 2011, he was elected to the board of directors for TechBridge, an Atlanta-based nonprofit organization that helps other non-profits use technology to improve their capability to serve the community.

Ferro earned both his BA in political science and his MBA from the University of Georgia. He continues to be involved with his alma mater, both as a mentor for young alumni and as a member of the alumni board of directors for the Terry College of Business. He lives in the metro Atlanta area with his three sons.

*   *   *

Michael Fitz is vice president of business solutions for Sprint. In this role, he is responsible for strategy and planning for Sprint's *Enterprise Solutions* business unit, including marketing and product management of business products ranging from wireline and cloud to M2M. He also manages Sprint's nationwide team of sales engineers who are responsible for selling, designing, and implementing solutions across the entire wireless, wireline, cloud, and M2M portfolio. Fitz also oversees Sprint's wireline business and manages Sprint's Emergency Response Team and In-Building Wireless Solutions teams.

Prior to his current position, he was the vice president of Solution Engineering and the Wireline Business Unit within the Sales and Distribution organization of Sprint. As Sprint's leader of the Wireline Business Unit, he oversaw the P&L as well as the various functions responsible for selling, designing, building, and servicing Sprint's $4 billion wireline product portfolio. Fitz has 20 years of experience with Sprint, including various customer service and product management roles. He has been awarded several Sprint annual executive leadership awards and has received industry awards including being named Fierce Telecom's "2013 Rising Star of Wireline." Prior to joining Sprint, he worked at GE.

Fitz was awarded his MBA from the University of Maryland and earned his bachelor's degree from Bucknell University. He serves as chairman of the board of directors for National Safe Place, a nationwide nonprofit providing services for runaway and homeless youth. He and his family reside in Leesburg, Virginia.

* * *

John Foley has spent nearly a decade sharing practical and inspirational messages on high performance with audiences around the world. The former lead solo pilot for the famed Blue Angels flight-demonstration squadron is among the most sought after conference speakers, presenting keynote messages at more than 100 events a year. He also is the founder and CEO of CenterPoint Companies, which provides in-depth training on the "how" of high performance. Foley is also the founder of the Glad To Be Here® Foundation, which administers a giving-forward program that partners with clients to make donations to worthy charities.

Foley's journey from an awe-struck child at an air show to the cockpit of the Blue Angels' F/A-18 Hornet aircraft is a study in persistence, hard work, and the will to overcome obstacles and setbacks. Those ideals fit within three overriding traits that mark Foley's presentations: First, a contagious attitude of thankfulness that he calls Glad To Be Here®. Second, an energizing delivery that inspires high performance and service to others. And, third, a practical model for living out his message that works in other organizations as well as it works for the Blue Angels.

Foley graduated from the US Naval Academy with a degree in mechanical engineering. He also was a defensive back for the Midshipmen, playing in two bowl games and helping Navy to one of the best four-year records in its football history. As a pilot, Foley was a "Top Ten Carrier Pilot" six times before becoming a Marine Corps instructor pilot and a Blue Angel. He holds master's degrees in business management from the Stanford Graduate School of Business (as a Sloan Fellow); in international policy studies from Stanford University; and in strategic studies from the Naval War College.

* * *

Stephen J. Gold is the senior vice president and chief information officer for CVS Caremark. In this role since July 2012, Gold is the company's senior technology executive, with responsibility for all information systems and technology operations, including information technology strategy, application development, and technology infrastructure.

A seasoned executive with more than 30 years of information systems management experience, he was previously senior vice president and CIO for Avaya, guiding all aspects of the company's technology strategy, as well as leading IT business operations and systems globally.

Prior to joining Avaya, Gold was the executive vice president, chief information officer, and corporate chief technology officer for GSI Commerce. At GSI, Steve was responsible for product development, product marketing, systems architecture, product engineering, and technology operations for one of the nation's premier eCommerce solutions providers, supporting brands such as Toys R Us, Polo, BCBG, Estee Lauder, Kate Spade, and all major sports leagues. He was also the divisional CIO at Merck & Co., for its Human Health and Vaccine businesses, and CIO at Medco Health Solutions, where he was the founder and general manager of Medco.Com.

Gold holds an undergraduate degree in computer science from Saint John's University. He has received numerous professional honors and has served on the boards of advisers for Hewlett-Packard and St. John's University.

* * *

Roger Gurnani serves as the chief information officer and executive vice president of Verizon Communications Inc. He has extensive experience with information technology and the telecommunications industry. He served as a senior vice president of Product Development of Cellco Partnership, Inc. (a/k/a Verizon Wireless Inc.) since April 2009. Gurnani served as president of West Area of Cellco Partnership, Inc. from 2005 to 2008. He served as vice president of information systems and chief information officer of Cellco Partnership from April 2000 to 2008. He served as vice president and chief information officer of Bell Atlantic Mobile from April 1997 to April 2000. Prior to joining Bell Atlantic Mobile, he served as executive director of broadband systems with Bell Atlantic from October 1994 to April 1997. Prior to that, he held a number of information technology positions at WilTel (now WorldCom). In 1996, he received WilTel's chairman's recognition award for the implementation of the world's first ATM-based Switched Digital Video network in Dover Township, New Jersey. He has worked in the transportation and manufacturing industries. Gurnani holds a bachelor's degree in industrial engineering and a master's in systems engineering from Auburn University.

*   *   *

Doug Harr is the chief information officer at Splunk. He is responsible for the deployment and management of technology at the company. He and his team serve Splunk's information technology needs using private and public cloud solutions, while managing web functionality and global facilities. Harr oversees corporate analytics, an internal Splunk implementation to deliver web analytics, application management, security forensics, and operational intelligence for the company at large.

He has been leading IT organizations for most of his career, at companies such as Ingres Corporation, Portal Software, and Hewlett-Packard. The rest of the time he has been in the IT consulting field, focused on delivering enterprise business applications to clients and technology companies like Symantec, VMware, and Activision.

Harr holds a BS degree in business from Cal Poly, SLO. He is engaged in the CISE CIO consortium, lectures at several local universities, and is a faculty member for the CIO Executive Development Program at San Francisco State University.

* * *

Patty Hatter is the senior vice president of operations and CIO for McAfee, a global computer security software company headquartered in Santa Clara, California. A duel-role leader, she has led an aggressive, transformational effort that drives enhanced IT and operations effectiveness and scalability across a global organization. She applies dynamic innovation while establishing strategic solutions to support a sustainable operations and infrastructure. Her responsibilities are to drive and empower cross-functional partnerships that align to achieve real, bottom-line profitability. A key to Hatter's success, enterprise-wide and both in her operations and IT teams, is vigorous employee engagement and global collaboration. Vision, passion, and a "can-do" mindset from her and her teams contribute to solidifying the organization's effectiveness and ability to consistently deliver tangible IT and process solutions for the business.

Recognized as an agent for change, Hatter joined McAfee in late 2010 with extensive leadership experience in a wide range of operations at Fortune 500 companies in the tech, telecommunications, financial services, and healthcare industries. She previously served as vice president of business operations at Cisco, where she reported to the heads of operations and channels, drove tighter integration, and improved productivity and performance between Cisco and the channel partners. Prior to Cisco, she worked more than 15 years at AT&T where she held executive positions in strategic planning, business development, and managing the professional services business unit within the United States and Europe.

Hatter holds a BS and an MS in mechanical engineering from Carnegie-Mellon University. She also attended executive education programs at Columbia University and Northwestern University. She resides in Northern California with her husband and son.

* * *

Shawn Henry is the president of CrowdStrike Services and CSO and a retired executive assistant director of the FBI. Henry, who served in three FBI field offices and at the bureau's headquarters, is credited with boosting the FBI's computer crime and cybersecurity investigative capabilities. He oversaw computer crime investigations spanning the globe, including denial-of-service attacks, bank and corporate breaches, and state-sponsored intrusions. He posted FBI cyberexperts in police agencies around the world, including the Netherlands, Romania, Ukraine, and Estonia.

He has appeared on *60 Minutes, CBS Evening News, Good Morning America, The Today Show, Dateline, Rock Center with Brian Williams,* and C-SPAN. He has been interviewed by *Forbes, BusinessWeek, The Wall Street Journal,* the Associated Press, and *USA Today.*

Henry earned a bachelor's degree in business administration from Hofstra University and a master's degree in criminal justice administration from Virginia Commonwealth University.

* * *

Jeanette Horan is a managing director at IBM and the company's former chief information officer. She led the development and implementation of a technology strategy in close partnership with the business. The IT organization provides innovative capabilities for IBM's workforce, drives IT operational excellence for the enterprise, and supports IBM's transformation agenda with a focus on the confluence of social, mobile, cloud, and analytics; and how to use these technologies securely to personalize and enhance employee and client experiences.

Previously, she was the vice president of Enterprise Business Transformation. In this role, Horan led IBM's transformation program for key back office processes to accelerate IBM's leadership as a globally integrated enterprise. In partnership with IBM's Global Business Services and SAP, she led a multidisciplinary, global team deploying simplified business processes worldwide.

She joined IBM in 1998 and has held leadership positions within the Lotus brand, Information Management, and IBM Software Group Strategy. Prior to joining the CIO office in 2006, Horan was responsible for worldwide product development for the information management business in Software Group, and was the general manager of IBM's Silicon Valley Laboratory.

Prior to joining Lotus, she spent four years with Digital Equipment Corporation, where she was vice president of development for the AltaVista business, bringing the Web search engine and suite of intranet products to market. She has more than 25 years of experience in development and management roles in the computer industry.

As part of her business and personal involvement in the advancement of technology and service to the community, Horan serves on the board of Microvision Inc., an innovative display and imaging solutions company. She also serves as a director on the board of Jane Doe No More Inc., an organization committed to improving the way society responds to victims of sexual assault.

A native of the United Kingdom, Horan earned a bachelor's degree in mathematics from the University of London and an MBA from Boston University.

* * *

Bask Iyer is chief information officer and senior vice president of technology & business operations at Juniper

Network, where he oversees operations that support a $4.4 billion global networking innovation company. With more than 25 years of experience in international business and IT management, he has strategically applied his business and technical expertise across large global companies, using technology as a transformational catalyst and growth driver.

Since joining Juniper in mid-2011, he sponsored two key programs to champion enterprise IT needs and better support the business, including Juniper on Juniper and Customer #1. His role was recently expanded to include business transformation, global business services, IT, and real estate workplace services, all critical services for Juniper's long-term success.

He joined Juniper from Honeywell, where he was company-wide CIO, leading transformation programs for both IT and many global functions. Earlier in his career, he was CIO at GlaxoSmithKline Beecham and held senior positions at Johnson & Johnson and CTS Corporation.

Iyer holds a bachelor's degree in mechanical engineering from Annamalai University in India and a master's degree in computer science from Florida Institute of Technology.

* * *

Sheila Jordan was appointed Symantec's chief information officer in February 2014. In this role, she is responsible for driving the company's information technology strategy and operations with a focus on building and supporting the global information technology effort.

Prior to joining Symantec, Jordan spent nine years at Cisco, where she served as senior vice president of IT, communication, and collaboration. She was responsible for delivering and integrating key IT services for Cisco's global workforce, including the development of the company's WebEx Social Collaboration platform, as well as the deployment of all emerging technologies. She also led mobility services and desktop strategy, in addition to launching an eStore for mobile that provides transactional applications.

Previously, Jordan held leadership roles at Grand Circle Corporation, as chief information officer and executive vice president, where she was responsible for developing the company's technical strategy, and at The Walt Disney Company, where she was a senior vice president for Destination Disney and vice president of marketing and sales finance. She was also a senior financial analyst at Martin Marietta, a construction supplies aggregate company.

Outside of work, she is a frequent speaker on topics addressing collaboration, mobility, Bring Your Own Device (BYOD) issues, and women's leadership. She also serves as a director for NextSpace, a provider of innovative physical and virtual infrastructure for entrepreneurs, and sits on the CIO Advisory Board for SnapLogic.

She received her bachelor's degree in accounting from the University of Central Florida and a master's degree in business administration from the Florida Institute of Technology.

*   *   *

Bruce Leidal is the chief information officer at Carestream, a $2.5 billion worldwide provider of medical and dental imaging systems and IT solutions; X-ray imaging systems for nondestructive testing; and advanced materials for the precision films and electronics markets with over 8,000 employees. He leads Carestream's global Information Technology (IT) organization, focusing on streamlining business processes and providing information that enables Carestream to optimize its business while continually improving its customers' experience.

Carestream has seen significant improvements in IT under Leidal's leadership, including: the establishment of a new IT Leadership team; significant upgrade of the IT talent pool; transformation of the business through successful implementation of over 100 major projects; simplification of the business through the consolidation and elimination of over 300 core applications; improvement of global IT operations through outsourcing; consolidation of applications development from locations in 28 countries to four Centers of Excellence; and reduction of overall IT cost to benchmark levels, yielding over $17 million in recurring annual savings while improving services.

The accomplishments of the IT transformation at Carestream have been recognized externally, including: a case study on talent acquisition published in Topgrading by Dr. Bradford Smart; a case study by the Society of Information Managers (SIM) Advanced Practice Council entitled, "IT Leadership at Carestream: Handling a Large Scale Divestiture"; and on Forbes.com, "There's A Smarter Way To Tighten An IT Budget", by Peter High.

Prior to joining Carestream, Leidal served as CIO of Hayes Lemmerz International (HLI), a $2.4 billion global automotive supplier for which he was responsible for transforming the IT function. His accomplishments led to improved information accuracy, streamlined decision making, and stronger business management. Previously, he held executive positions at Systems Thinking, General Motors, and Federal-Mogul Corporation. He was a management consult at AT Kearney and gained his managerial and technical expertise while at EDS and Texas Instruments.

Leidal received a BS in information systems from Madonna University in Livonia, Michigan, and has several certifications including Project Management Professional (PMP) from the Project Management Institute and IT Management from Learning Tree International.

* * *

Ralph Loura recently joined Hewlett-Packard as chief information officer for Enterprise Group and Global Sales

Operations. A believer in IT's ability to drive business outcomes, his objective is to help shape go-to-market strategies through world-class processes, tools, and data that identify opportunities for HP's Enterprise Group. Loura advocates tight integration with the user community to identify underlying business needs and deliver simple, straightforward, user-friendly solutions while driving operational simplicity and removing complexity and cost.

He comes to HP after several years as senior vice president and chief information officer of the Clorox Company where he took IT from an underperforming cost center to an organization that is closely involved with supporting company strategy. He came with a wealth of experience and an understanding of the enterprise systems space, having served in IT leadership roles at Cisco, Symbol, and AT&T Bell Laboratories. In 2012, *Computerworld* named Loura one of its 2012 Premier 100 IT leaders; and in 2013, *Consumer Goods Technology* named him CIO of the Year.

He holds an MS in computer science from Northwestern University and a BS in computer science-mathematics from Saint Joseph's College. HP creates new possibilities for technology to have a meaningful impact on people, businesses, governments, and society. With the broadest technology portfolio spanning printing, personal systems, software, services, and IT infrastructure, HP delivers solutions for customers' most complex challenges in every region of the world.

*   *   *

Robert Lux was named senior vice president and chief information officer of Freddie Mac in 2010. He is a member of the company's senior operating committee and reports directly to the CEO. He is responsible for the company's information technology assets and services. In this capacity, he oversees end-to-end technology solutions that ensure delivery of strong operational platforms and integrated services throughout Freddie Mac's businesses.

Prior to coming to Freddie Mac, Lux was a principal at Towers Watson, a leading global professional services company, where he was responsible for leading teams on three continents in the delivery of commercial risk modeling applications for the insurance industry. Prior to that, he was chief architect for GMAC Financial Services and CTO for GMAC Residential Capital. He also held IT leadership positions at EDS and Reuters.

Lux has more than 30 years' experience in the IT industry and more than 10 years' experience in the mortgage industry. He is a current member of the MBA's Residential Technology Steering Committee and earned the MBA's Certified Mortgage Technologist designation. He earned an MS in management of technology from the University of Pennsylvania and a BS in commerce and engineering from Drexel University.

*   *   *

Andi Mann is vice president of strategic solutions at CA Technologies. He is an accomplished information technologist with extensive global expertise. For over 25 years and across five continents, Mann has worked in technology for Fortune 500 corporations, technology vendors, governments, and as a leading analyst and consultant. He has been published in the *New York Times, USA Today, Forbes, CIO, Wall Street Journal*; presented worldwide on innovation, cloud, mobility, automation, and strategy; and has interviewed and hosted radio, television, Internet, and live events. He is co-author of the popular handbook, *Visible Ops—Private Cloud,* and a new book, *The Innovative CIO*. He blogs at http://pleasediscuss.com/andimann and tweets as @AndiMann http://twitter.com/andimann.

* * *

Israel Martinez is the national partner for Newport Board Group's Global Cyber Practice, Technology Strategy & Innovation. He is an expert at board-level strategies that minimize the balance sheet impact and personal risk of cyber compromises. He is DHS certified and internationally trained as an executive in cyber counterterrorism and defense and military-grade strategies that protect corporations and board member's personal digital-reputation. He's also a 2015 nominee as an NACD Fellow and recipient of the 2015 HITEC top 100 award as one of the most influential Hispanic technology executives in the United States.

Martinez is a recipient of the US Senatorial Medal of Freedom (also awarded to Ronald Reagan and General Schwarzkopf) and a board member to Globes International (Tel Aviv's "WSJ"), the National Healthcare Information Sharing and Analysis Center (established under Executive Order of the US president), the Global Institute for Cyber

Security Research at NASA KSC, the National Cyber Security Council, the Axon Global Alliance (specializing in cyber counter intelligence), and the Wider Net (dedicated to advancing cognitive diversity in Fortune 500 boards).

He is also an accomplished thought leader and speaker, appearing in the WSJ MarketWatch®, NACD® Annual Board Leadership Conferences, DHS Office of Analysis & Intelligence, Forbes CEO Conferences, *CIO Magazine*, US Federal Reserve, US Congress, Department of Defense, and the Globes International Leadership Conferences (as an anchor speaker after Prime Minister Netanyahu).

* * *

Gerri Martin-Flickinger is senior vice president and chief information officer at Adobe. She oversees Adobe's global information technology team, providing strategic direction and management for the company's IT infrastructure worldwide, including its hosted services. In partnership with the business, Martin-Flickinger also has responsibility for developing innovative enterprise solutions built with Adobe products and technologies that solve business issues and help drive Adobe's business.

She has more than 20 years of experience leading large-scale global IT organizations for companies experiencing explosive growth. Before joining Adobe, Martin-Flickinger was CIO of VeriSign, CIO for Network Associates, and held several senior systems roles at Chevron Corporation.

* * *

Tim McCabe is former chief information officer and senior vice president of Delphi. He joined Delphi in 2006 as director of strategy and sourcing within the Information Technology division. In this role, he led restructuring activities as well as the deployment of the global supplier management organization.

Prior to joining Delphi, McCabe worked at General Motors, where he served in a variety of leadership positions, including lead director of global outsourcing. Before joining GM, he also worked in the insurance industry focusing on commercial risk and litigation.

He has served on the Conference Board's Executive Council on Outsourcing and Offshoring, is recognized as an expert in the subject of IT sourcing and outsourcing, and is a frequent speaker in business and information technology–related forums. McCabe also serves on the Finance Committee for the City Council in his community. He has a bachelor's degree in philosophy from Oakland University and a master's degree in management from Walsh College.

* * *

Eric J. McNulty holds an appointment as director of Research and Professional Programs and Program Faculty at the National Preparedness Leadership Initiative (NPLI), a joint program of the Harvard School of Public Health and the Center for Public Leadership at Harvard's Kennedy School of Government. He is an instructor at the Harvard School of Public Health. His work with the program centers on leadership in high-stakes, high-stress situations. He is currently working on a book based on meta-leadership, the core leadership framework of the NPLI curriculum.

McNulty is the principal author of the NPLI's case studies on leadership decision making in the Boston Marathon bombing response, innovation in the response to Hurricane Sandy, and the professional/political interface in the Deepwater Horizon response, drawing on his firsthand research as well as extensive interviews with leaders involved in the responses.

He is the co-author, along with Dr. Leonard Marcus and Dr. Barry Dorn, of the second edition of *Renegotiating Health Care: Resolving Conflict to Build Collaboration* (Jossey-Bass, 2011). He is co-author of a chapter on meta-leadership in the *McGraw-Hill Homeland Security Handbook* (2012).

McNulty is a widely published business author, speaker, researcher, and thought leadership strategist. McNulty writes a regular online column for *Strategy + Business* and is a contributing editor to *Business Review* (China) and the Center for Higher Ambition Leadership. He has written multiple articles for the *Harvard Business Review (HBR)* as well as articles for *Harvard Management Update, Strategy and Innovation, Marketwatch, the Boston Business Journal,* and *Worthwhile* magazine, among others. His HBR cases have been anthologized through the HBR paperback series and have been used in business education curricula in the United States and as far away as France and the Philippines.

McNulty co-founded Harvard Business Publishing's conference business and served as its director for six years.

He produced thought leadership events around the world, working with some of the most celebrated executives and management experts. He also developed custom programs in collaboration with leading companies such as Accenture, Coca-Cola, SAS, UPS, Visa, and others. He is a frequent speaker and moderator at business events.

Previously, McNulty held management roles at Bloomingdale's, Mark Cross, European Travel & Life magazine, Wilgus Advertising, Trans National Group, Cybersmith, and Learningsmith. His specialty was marketing communications.

McNulty holds a bachelor's degree in economics (with honors) from the University of Massachusetts at Amherst (1981) and a Master's degree in Leadership from Lesley University. In this program he explored leadership as it relates to climate change, urbanization, and other high consequence global trends.

* * *

Chris Miller is chief information officer at Avanade, where he is responsible for the leadership, management, and implementation of the technology capabilities that power the company's 20,000 professionals across more than 25 countries. He champions IT as the fabric that connects Avanade's innovative business thinkers, technical subject matter experts, and transformative technology solutions. This fabric of people, tools, and ideas enables the company to deliver large-scale solutions to its customers in every major industry.

He and his team work closely with Microsoft to maintain Avanade's role as an aggressive early adopter of Microsoft enterprise technologies. He regularly shares firsthand experience and insights about deployments with customers to help them optimize their own operations.

Prior to joining Avanade, Miller spent 16 years at Accenture, where he had multiple leadership roles. He directed large, solution-oriented projects for global retail and pharmaceutical clients. In his last assignment, he led a multiyear initiative to enable 200,000 global employees with next-generation collaboration capabilities.

*   *   *

Steve Phillips is senior vice president and chief information officer for Avnet, Inc., reporting to Avnet's CEO. He is also a member of the Avnet executive board and a corporate officer.

He came to Avnet with the 2005 acquisition of Memec, where he had served as senior vice president and chief information officer since 2004. Prior to joining Memec, he was senior vice president and chief information officer for Gateway Inc. He joined Gateway in 1999 and served as vice president of information technology (IT) in London and San Diego before his appointment in 2003 to chief information officer.

Between 1996 and 1999, Phillips worked for Diageo, the international food and drinks group, where he was the IT director for its European foods division. He previously spent eight years in a variety of leadership roles at Thorn EMI, a UK defense-electronics company.

Under his IT leadership, Avnet has been recognized with multiple IT awards, including CIO100, InformationWeek Elite 100, and InfoWorld Green 15. Additionally, Phillips received an HMG Strategy Transformational CIO Leadership Award in 2012. In 2011, *Computerworld* named him a "Premier 100 IT Leader." This lifetime recognition honors executives for exceptional technology leadership, innovative ideas that address business challenges, and effectively managing IT strategies.

Phillips is chairman of the board at Wick Communications, a news and specialty publications company. From 2008 through 2011, he served as chairman of the board of the Arizona Technology Council, a trade association that connects, represents, and supports Arizona's technology industry.

He holds a BSc (Hons) in electronic engineering from Essex University and a post-graduate diploma in management studies from Thames Valley University. He is a Fellow of the Institution of Engineering & Technology.

* * *

Ken Piddington is chief information officer (CIO) and executive adviser at MRE Consulting. He is an experienced business leader and technology strategist with more than

15 years of transformation leadership experience gained as CIO and executive adviser for Fortune 500 companies in North America and Europe.

Piddington uses his extensive experience in people leadership, business operations, and technology innovation to partner with CIOs, CXOs, and their leadership teams to help them develop effective plans and strategies to achieve meaningful results in their respective businesses. He was the CIO at Global Partners LP, a Fortune 500 midstream logistics and energy products marketing company, where he was responsible for leading, developing, and implementing the business technology strategy during four years of unprecedented growth where the company revenues grew from $6 billion to $20 billion. This included the successful integration of multiple acquisitions and the implementation of supply chain technologies necessary to support dramatic geographic and line of business expansion.

His successful track record as a business leader and technology strategist includes serving as partner at Lyland Associates, Inc., where he managed the business technology division of the company's energy practice. In this role, he served as a technology adviser and led custom development and application implementation projects for its Fortune 500 clients.

Piddington is recognized as an industry thought leader, is a regular speaker at business and association conferences, and has been featured in multiple media publications. He has served on the board of trustees for the Sage School in

Massachusetts and on the leadership board for the MIT CIO Leadership Institute. He has also served as a mentor in the CIO Executive Council's Pathways program.

* * *

Greg Roberts is a managing director in Accenture's Communications, Media, and Technology practice. He is responsible for the global relationship with an IT Company for the past two and a half years and is accountable for approximately all Accenture personnel serving that client. With more than 20 years' experience, he has led significant business consulting, system integration, and IT outsourcing efforts at various Accenture clients within the communications, media and technology, public service, and products industries. He has helped reengineer large organizations to dramatically reduce operating costs and increase overall efficiency. Additionally, he has helped his clients adopt standard and consistent processes as well as consolidate systems and operations following major acquisitions.

* * *

Kevin Sealy is CIO practice head and partner at Korn/ Ferry Whitehead Mann in London. He has 30 years of experience in the information technology industry. He specializes in appointing senior information technology professionals across all industry sectors, and has worked with many leading companies on high-profile chief information officer–related placements.

In his previous position as a partner in IBM Business Consulting Services (formerly PricewaterhouseCoopers Consulting), he led the delivery of technology strategy and systems integration work with blue-chip clients internationally. His client consulting work focused on the management of the IT organization and the delivery of complex technology and systems projects, including program management, IT transformation, technology strategy, and IT management.

Sealy began his career as a graduate trainee in the IT department at Mobil Oil Company Ltd. His MS in physics is from Oxford University. He is a member of the Institute of Business Consulting (MIBC) and a certified management consultant (CMC).

* * *

Frank Slootman has served as ServiceNow's president and chief executive officer, and as a director, since May 2, 2011. Prior to joining ServiceNow, Slootman served as a partner with Greylock Partners, a venture capital firm from January 2011 to April 2011, and served as an adviser to EMC Corporation from January 2011 to February 2012.

From July 2009 to January 2011, he served as president of the Backup Recovery Systems Division at EMC. From July 2003 to July 2009, Slootman served as president and chief executive officer of Data Domain, Inc., a data storage solution company, which was acquired by EMC in 2009. As the CEO of Data Domain, he blazed new trails creating a high-growth enterprise storage company that went public on NASDAQ in 2007.

Prior to joining Data Domain, he served as an executive at Borland Software Corporation from June 2000 to June 2003, most recently as senior vice president of products. From March 1993 to June 2000, he held consecutive general management positions for two enterprise software divisions of Compuware Corporation. Slootman holds undergraduate and graduate degrees in Economics from the Netherlands School of Economics, Erasmus University Rotterdam.

*   *   *

Dave Smoley assumed his current position as chief information officer for AstraZeneca in 2013. Previously, he was chief information officer and senior vice president for Flextronics International Ltd., serving there since 2006. Prior to Flextronics, he served in various roles at Honeywell, including chief information officer and vice president of Honeywell's Aerospace Electronics Systems.

Before joining Honeywell, he was vice president and limited partner for Lovett Miller & Co., Venture Capital. Smoley has held various management positions with General Electric, including the position of chief information officer and director for GE Power Controls in Barcelona, Spain. His extensive information technology career also includes various IT positions with J.P. Morgan. He holds a BS in Computer Science from Clemson University and an MBA from the University of Virginia.

* * *

Tim Stanley founded and is the president/CEO of Tekexecs, Innovatects, and CXOCo—a complementary set of business strategy, innovation, talent, and technology-focused advisory services and equity investment for select growth companies. He is also actively involved in several public and private company board of directors and advisory roles, and as an angel and venture capital investor in a variety of innovative companies. Stanley is also an adjunct professor at the Merage School of Business at UCI, where he created and co-teaches EDGE, a Capstone MBA/Exec MBA course focused on globalization, innovation, and technology as strategic catalysts for business transformation.

He has also been active in launching and leading the Center for Digital Transformation (CDT) at the University of California Irvine (UCI), which brings industry-leading CXOs, innovative startups, and renowned academic experts together to explore the strategies, opportunities, and challenges facing business leaders in a more technology dependent and digitally driven world.

Stanley was named *Information Week*'s "Chief of the Year" for his unique innovation, business and IT roles, and achievements. He has also been recognized as one of *InfoWorld*'s

"Top 25 CTOs," *Interactive Week*'s "Top 25 Unsung Heroes of the Internet," and received CIO's "100 Innovators Award" and CIO Insight's "Partners in Alignment" award for his successful linkage of business strategy and technology. He has also received multiple "CIO 100" awards; *Computerworld*'s "Best Places to Work in IT" for nine consecutive years; and the American Business Awards "Best MIS & IT Organization."

He holds an MBA in international business and technology management from the Thunderbird Graduate School of Management and Arizona State University, and a BS degree in engineering from the University of Washington. Stanley is also an alumni of the AACSB Bridge program to prepare executives for academia, and other professional and executive education programs at Stanford, MIT, and Babson. He has lived, worked, and traveled extensively throughout the United States, Europe, Latin America, and Asia throughout his career, and after the 2014 HMG Summit embarked on another extended trip to Europe, the Middle East, and Asia.

* * *

Patrick Steele is former executive vice president and CIO for Delta Dental of California and a member of the senior executive management team. Delta Dental is part of a $7 billion enterprise and one of the largest dental benefit administrators in the nation.

He has 47 years of experience in healthcare, insurance, corporate retail, wholesale, supply chain, merchandising, information technology (IT), dot.com profit & loss, and worldwide retail exchange functions. Prior to joining Delta Dental, he was involved in consulting and business development, and was active in establishing several technology companies that serve the retail sector. As a former member of the executive management team for a $37 billion retailer, Steele led numerous strategic projects, inclusive of both large and small mergers and acquisitions. He sits on the advisory board for a venture capital firm and is active in the evaluation of new companies for the firm to invest in. He is also a board member of Dignity Health, a large, multistate healthcare delivery company based in San Francisco.

Steele holds a BA in business administration and a BS in mathematics, both from the University in Washington. He has been active in numerous civic organizations.

*   *   *

Cynthia Stoddard is NetApp's chief information officer (CIO) and senior vice president. As CIO of NetApp, she is leading and evolving the IT organization for the new digital era. Her responsibilities involve driving the traditional IT functions that include providing a long-term technology vision that supports and aligns with the company's goals and strategies, business plans, operating requirements, and improving overall efficiencies. In addition, she is evolving IT to deliver business value beyond traditional boundaries by focusing on innovation, customer adaptive practices, and strategic partnerships.

As a senior executive of NetApp, Stoddard is providing thought leadership on industry, business, and product direction. She is known as a customer-facing CIO—leading IT to enable NetApp customers to succeed. Additionally, she is the executive sponsor for the NetApp-on-NetApp initiative to increase awareness that NetApp is an IT leader. She recently won the 2014 *Computerworld* Premier 100 IT Leaders Award and was named *Huffington Post*'s Top 100 Most Social CIOs. Under her leadership, NetApp IT has been recognized in the Information Week 500 (2012 & 2013) and the Information Elite 100 (2014).

Stoddard has more than 25 years of business experience and IT expertise leading large global organizations in supply chain, retail, and technology companies. Before joining NetApp in 2010, she was group vice president of information technology at Safeway Inc. and was recognized as one of the Top Women in Grocery and also a Woman of Influence in the Food Industry. Other positions she has held include group CIO for NOL Group, the parent of APL Ltd., a global transportation and logistics company, as well as executive roles in other global transportation companies. While she was CIO at NOL Group, the organization was named in the Top 100 of *Information Week*'s Top 500 innovative users of technology for four successive years.

She holds a bachelor of science degree in accounting from Western New England University, from which she graduated cum laude, and an MBA from Marylhurst University.

* * *

Clif Triplett is managing partner at SteelPointe Partners, LLP. He is a senior executive with broad and in-depth experience and knowledge of nearly all facets of information technology on a global basis. He has significant experience with Fortune 200 companies and industry leaders in the oilfield services, tractor, automotive, aerospace, defense, and telecommunication industries. He is a respected leader, innovator, and change agent with keen ability to quickly assess a situation and create a strategy and architecture that best serves the need of the particular company.

Triplett has developed and driven market and internal strategic initiatives for major enterprises, start-ups, turnarounds, divestitures, mergers, and acquisitions. He is a leader acknowledged for integrity, strategic thinking, architectural strength, operational excellence, manufacturing expertise, information security, and global business acumen.

*   *   *

Dave Wright is chief strategy officer for ServiceNow. In this role, he is responsible for working with internal and external resources to establish areas of expansion and directional strategies for ServiceNow. Dave has more than 20 years experience in the IT industry, specifically within virtualization, cloud infrastructure, service management, performance management, data center automation, and software development. Prior to joining ServiceNow in 2010, Wright spent over six years with VMware as vice president of technical services for EMEA, where he was responsible for all pre-sales, professional services, training, and technical account management delivery across this region. He also headed up the technical division for Northern and Southern Europe for Mercury Interactive and spent six years at Peregrine Systems, where he held a variety of senior technical and marketing positions. Previously, he worked for Boole & Babbage (BMC) and Candle Services (IBM).

ABOUT THE AUTHOR

Hunter Muller is president and chief executive officer of HMG Strategy, LLC, a global IT strategy consulting firm based in Westport, Connecticut. Mr. Muller has more than three decades of experience in business strategy consulting. His primary focus is IT organization development, leadership, and business alignment. His concepts and programs have been used successfully by premier corporations worldwide to improve executive performance, enhance collaboration, elevate the role of IT, and align enterprise strategy across the topmost levels of management. He lives in Fairfield, Connecticut, with his wife and their two children.

ABOUT HMG STRATEGY LLC

At HMG Strategy, LLC, our passion is helping chief information officers (CIOs) be transformational executives and leaders. No environment and job changes faster than the role of the CIO. Twenty years ago, the role of CIO didn't even exist, and today it is one of the most important hires a chief executive officer and board can make. At HMG Strategy, we focus on providing CIOs with the leadership strategies, resources, and services you need to make IT a strategic differentiator for your company, make yourself strategic to your C-suite peers, and make the connections you need to accelerate your career. We are dedicated to our CIO community.

In our international network of over 70,000, we have global CIO and senior IT leaders who actively engage in our programs, set the agenda for our research, and share their leadership strategies to help other CIOs be successful. We are the strongest CIO network in the world.

Our CIO Executive Leadership Summits are a favorite among CIOs and IT leaders. CIOs network and share real-world experiences in a professional and relaxed setting. Our events are also a great opportunity for CIOs to build relationships and gain insights from the top CIO search firms.

We are a global network dedicated to professional success and ascent.

For details on HMG Strategy, to sign up for our newsletter, or to register for upcoming events, visit www .hmgstrategy.com

INDEX

233